THE CONFIDENT TEEN

A PRACTICAL GUIDE TO BOOST YOUR CONFIDENCE, TRANSFORM YOUR SELF-WORTH, AND TAKE CONTROL OF YOUR LIFE

MARNIE DAVID

Disclaimer

CONTENTS

FREE SELF REFLECTION JOURNAL!
The 10 Best Journal Prompts to Unlock Your Authentic
Self!

Download my journal freebie to get a head start on
understanding and accepting yourself for who you are.

INTRODUCTION

Picture this: it's a bright summer's day, and everywhere you look, the world seems to shine with endless possibilities.

The air is filled with the sound of laughter and carefree joy, especially from a group of giggling ten-year-olds nearby. Their energy and giddiness are tangible. Yet, amid the backdrop of your bustling thoughts, you can't help but find them ... annoying.

Wait a minute, you think, feeling a jolt of alarm and introspection. *Wasn't that me not too long ago? Why didn't I notice how exasperating I was? But it's just innocent laughter ... Why am I so bothered by this, anyway?!*

Then it hits you: you're standing at a one-way threshold. Sweet independence is calling, and the weight of expectation is growing a little heavier every day. As the sun's rays warm your skin, a burning question fills every cell in your body.

When does a kid become an adult?

I remember contemplating that same question when I was a teen. It was especially bad one afternoon when I was so upset, I just had to get away from everyone and everything. After a long walk, I plopped onto a bench in the park.

"Long day?"

The voice came from the other side of the bench and belonged to a man with years and years etched into his face. He had the gentlest eyes and a smile that seemed to hold all the answers.

"You know," he said as if he could hear the questions running rampant in my mind, "when I was a kid, I had heard the words 'Now you're a real man' so many times. My first hunting trip, the day I got my driver's license . . . The time I told my brother I had kissed a girl for the first time!"

We shared a chuckle.

"But as I got older, the issue weighed heavier and heavier on me. Then, on my fifteenth birthday, I finally mustered up the courage to ask my mom when I would *officially* be an adult. And you'll never believe it, but . . ."

I leaned forward, eager to soak in his wisdom.

"This morning I woke up and I just can't seem to remember the exact moment I became an adult!"

I frowned, pursing my lips as I tried to ignore his infectious laughter this time.

"But don't worry," he continued, his eyes full of reassurance, "you're already on the train, and it's going to be an interesting ride from here on out. There will be unimaginable experiences, there will be bumps, and there will be important stops along the way—but none of them will be *the moment*."

"I don't get it," I grumbled.

The man leaned back on the bench, his gaze drifting to the distant horizon of nostalgia. "Adulthood isn't marked by some grand milestone. It's a journey of learning from your mistakes, embracing responsibility, and cultivating the qualities that will turn you into the person you want to be."

He turned to me. "Want to know the secret to it all?"

I nodded.

"I'll tell you. But only if you promise to pass it on one day."

"I promise."

He smiled. "Confidence."

"That's it?"

"Sure! It's the armor that shields you from doubt, the fuel that propels you forward . . . no matter what, and the light that guides your path."

To be honest, it sounded easy—totally within my reach, you know? What the man didn't tell me, what I had to discover for myself is that like anything worthwhile in life, it takes deliberate practice to build confidence. No matter where you come from, what school you attend, what classes you take, what extracurricular activities you do, who you hang out with, or how popular you are, no one is born confident. Don't let anyone convince you otherwise, ever.

The transition from childhood to adulthood is exciting, but it's also littered with difficulties. And where you are right now, at this crossroads called adolescence, is especially challenging. In between getting to know yourself and developing your own values, beliefs, and interests, you have intense stuff to deal with . . .

- Dealing with your friends, making new ones, fitting in, and navigating all that social pressure.
- Getting good grades, taking extra classes, preparing for college entrance exams, and not to mention the extracurriculars.
- Being a good family member, even if you find those people annoying sometimes!
- Learning to accept and love yourself.

These things can cause some serious stress and make you unsure of yourself, which sucks because it only doubles the pressure. Yeah, I know *exactly* how you feel.

But you know what? It's OK. You're OK. Everything you're feeling and thinking is normal.

Think of your teenage years as life's boot camp. It's a rite of passage. And once you get to the other side, you'll have the skills to take on anything life can throw at you.

But all of us, no matter how old we are, need a little help.

I say this knowing that my teenage self is rolling her eyes at me. Because growing up, I wasn't exactly a fan of asking for help.

Despite learning the secret to taking control of my life from that kind man in the park, I didn't know how to implement it. My twin sister, Casey, had the whole confidence thing down, which just made things worse for me. While we were in school, I never asked her how she did it, because then I'd have to admit that I was scared and couldn't figure stuff out on my own. And so I pretended I was fine. I did many things to please my friends (and sometimes even my family) just to feel included. Whatever I did, I never let my guard down. But at night, alone in my bed, where no one could see me, I felt so alone and lost.

It took me ages to become a confident person. Now, I'd be lying if I said my teenage years were all bad, but I know for sure it would've been easier if I had the right tools and guidance (and the guts to ask for help).

When I became a teacher, I developed an intense desire to instill confidence in my students. I knew they'd have a massive advantage in life if they could face challenges with the confidence I never had as a teen. While brainstorming how I could teach them to be confident, I remembered my sister. So, after all those years, I finally asked Casey how she had managed to be so confident when we were growing up.

"Me? Confident?" She blushed. "Guess I faked it pretty well!"

Ha! I wasn't alone, after all.

But I didn't want my students to fake it. And, having welcomed my first son into the world, I certainly didn't want him to fake it. They all deserved better, and I wanted them to use that secret ingredient to their full advantage. So, I started coming up with creative ways to teach my students everything I had learned about the art of building confidence. Day by day, I saw the positive impact it had on them. You, too, deserve to live with confidence and an unshakable sense of self-worth. Your teenage years should be some of the *best* years of your life—not the easiest, but definitely among the best.

(Spoiler: Life doesn't get easier when you grow up. You just learn to deal with it like a pro. And confidence helps. Like, a lot!)

Whatever your personal circumstances, and whatever is holding you back, you should know you *can* overcome it. Seriously—I've worked with young people from all walks of life, and if there's one thing I've learned, it's that if you really want things to change, nothing in the world can stop you from making it happen.

You've already taken the first step toward more confidence and becoming a stronger, better you by reading this far. All you have to do to unlock your full potential is read on.

See you in Chapter One!

CHAPTER 1
UNDERSTANDING CONFIDENCE

"*Confidence isn't walking into a room thinking you're better than everyone. It's walking in and not having to compare yourself to anyone at all.*"

DWAYNE ('THE ROCK') JOHNSON

Sure sounds easy . . . Until you're in a room comparing yourself to your classmates, right?

After talking with that nice man in the park, I felt super sure of myself. And why wouldn't I? I had the secret to overcoming all the obstacles on my journey to adulthood: confidence, my new superpower.

But when I got home, uncertainty hit me like a roller-coaster drop. In just one afternoon, I was back to feeling insecure, and my self-doubt had grown even stronger by bedtime.

The struggle is real . . .

If self-doubt takes you on roller coaster rides, don't feel ashamed—it's totally normal. The good news is that you're not at the mercy of those roller coaster rides. With guidance, you can take control and become confident despite the doubt.

In this chapter, we'll unravel the mysteries surrounding confidence and debunk myths that might be holding you back. You'll gain the knowledge to navigate adolescence with self-assurance and learn to embrace and own your unique strengths, quirks, and imperfections with pride.

WHAT IS CONFIDENCE?

Have you ever studied really hard for a test and just *knew* you'd ace it? Or trained like crazy for a sports event or a competition and *knew* you had it in you to win?

That's confidence.

When you're confident, you feel sure of yourself and believe in your abilities, even in the face of tough challenges. You also take pride in your individuality and your actions show that you embrace your quirks. But it's not about acting superior. It's about saying, "I can do this," and genuinely believing it in your heart. It doesn't stop there, though. Confidence also involves acting on that belief in yourself.

The most important thing to remember about confidence is that it's a skill you can improve with practice by building a confident mindset, comparing yourself kindly (because we all have our unique talents!), and overcoming self-doubt.

Does being confident mean you'll never doubt yourself again?

Nope. Self-doubt will always find a way to creep in. Even the most confident people experience fear and uncertainty. Confidence just means pushing through and not allowing self-doubt to stop you from living life and being the best version of yourself.

RECAP: AN EASY EQUATION FOR DEFINING CONFIDENCE

Confidence = (Believe in your abilities + Embrace your individuality) + (Act on your belief in yourself) + (Push through, no matter what + Practice a confident mindset)

In short: C = (B+E) + (A) + (P+P)

Now, remember: Confidence means BEAPP up!

In other words: Confidence means believing in your abilities and embracing your individuality. When you're confident, you act on your beliefs, push through when things get tough, and practice a confident mindset every day.

WHAT CONFIDENCE IS NOT

Emily, an energetic 16-year-old, never had a shy bone in her body. Having a competitive spirit and being academically strong, she believed she could become a valuable member of the school's debate team. The team was impressed with how much she knew and welcomed her with enthusiasm. During the first debate, Emily dominated the conversation, often overpowering her opponents with her loud voice and strong opinions. The opposing team soon lost interest in the debate. And by the time it was all over, Emily's own team seemed distant and unimpressed with her clear win for them. Then the team leader approached her and said, "This isn't going to work out."

Confidence is not arrogance

Emily's story is a brilliant example of the fine line that exists between being confident and having an arrogance about you. Remember, confidence is a belief in yourself and what you can achieve. It's not a belief that you're better than others. True confidence is about being secure in yourself without diminishing the worth of your classmates or the people you meet. True confidence is lifting others up and recognizing their strengths, too.

Note: Being bold doesn't necessarily make you arrogant. The defining factor lies in how and why you use it, and

especially in how you treat other people while using bold-
ness to your advantage.

Confidence is not perfection

Don't waste your energy trying to be flawless or thinking
everyone expects you to have all the answers when you're
confident. True confidence is being able to smile and say,
"I don't have the answer, but I'll try my best to find it!" It's
about embracing your imperfections and believing in
yourself despite doubts and mistakes.

Confidence isn't dependent on external factors

It's easy to assume that confidence comes from things like
appearance, popularity, or achievements—but it doesn't.
While external validation like receiving praise when
helping others or getting good grades are useful indica-
tors that you're on the right track, they don't define you as
a confident person. The source of confidence lies inside
you, regardless of everything happening on the outside.

Confidence is not the absence of fear

Even the most confident people have fears, but they take
action despite them. That's because confidence is having
the courage to step outside of your comfort zone and
pursue your goals, even when it feels scary.

> "I used to be so afraid of public speaking that I would throw up before I went on stage. I would get so nervous that I would shake, and my voice would quiver. But I learned how to overcome my anxiety and now I love public speaking. I actually get energized by it."

> TONY ROBBINS

Confidence is unique

There's no blueprint for what a confident person looks like, or how they talk or act. Some people may be more outgoing and bolder, while others may be reserved and introspective, but they can be equally confident. Confidence is, after all, about being true to yourself and embracing your unique strengths and qualities.

RECAP: CONFIDENCE IS NOT...

Confidence is not arrogance, perfection, or a life without fear. It doesn't depend on outside factors but on what's inside of you. Finally, confidence looks different for everyone because we're all unique.

WHY DOES CONFIDENCE MATTER?

Confidence is the foundation you need to build a fulfilling life. It opens doors, propels you forward, and empowers you to live without limits. Let's explore specific areas of life where it pays to be confident.

Confidence helps you overcome fear and anxiety

How many times have you really, *really* wanted to do something but came up with a rock-solid excuse not to and regretted it afterward? Or how many times have you looked the other way to keep the peace despite seeing something wrong happening?

The above examples are classic results of fear and anxiety. Pretty annoying, right? This may come as a surprise, but fear and anxiety are actually good for you because they protect you in genuinely dangerous situations.

So, your mission is not to banish fear and anxiety altogether, but to understand when it's helpful and when it's just holding you back from living. Confidence is a powerful ally in helping you spot the difference, and it gives you the strength to overcome challenges and grow beyond your comfort zone.

Confidence makes you resilient in the face of challenges

It's one thing to overcome the fear of facing life's challenges, but after conquering the fear, what do you do when things go wrong?

Like, what do you do when your crush crushes your spirit by saying no after you ask them on a date? Or what do you do when the class bully snickers to mock you and influences your classmates to look at you funny when you're about to do a presentation?

A powerful byproduct of confidence is the ability to bounce back, shrug your shoulders, and march on with pride—better known as resilience. Sure, it's going to hurt if someone breaks your heart or tries to embarrass you, and sometimes it'll be difficult to complete tasks and push through challenges. But as a confident teen, you'll have the resilience to make things work—you'll either find a solution or walk away with your self-assurance intact when things don't work out.

Confidence helps you make the best of bad situations

My high school English teacher had a bright yellow class-room, and the walls were full of inspirational and motivational quotes. One of them was in the front of the classroom, right above the blackboard.

> "If you fail to plan, you plan to fail."

BENJAMIN FRANKLIN

Sound advice, but it can also make life harder than it needs to be if you don't add flexibility into the mix. That's because, sometimes, you can make the best and most well-thought-out plans, only to have life throw curveballs and shatter those plans.

> *"Life is what happens to you when you're busy making other plans."*
>
> JOHN LENNON

Plans don't always work out. And to keep your sanity, you need to be OK with that. Be flexible so you can adapt and find creative solutions. Confidence helps you to stay positive, make the best of the messes you might find yourself in, and turn challenges into opportunities.

Confidence gives you a better outlook on life

Imagine a confident you applying for your dream job or pursuing your passions. Just by believing in yourself and your abilities, you're already setting yourself apart from others and increasing your chances of success.

OK, so maybe you're not in the job market yet, but that's not the point. Confident people ooze all the right stuff to stand out. Whether you want to become the captain of your sports team, lead a school committee, get that part-time job you've been eyeing, or whatever your heart desires, your chance of being noticed and chosen is higher when you're confident.

Confidence helps you make choices that are good for you

Of all the things I had to shake off in life, my need to please people was one of the hardest. I felt like I had this obligation to be a good person, and if I didn't do the things people asked, it meant I was a terrible person and friend. Well, I later learned that saying no doesn't make you a bad person. It makes you confident, respectable, and dependable.

You have the right to make your own choices. So, say no to that party invitation, a day out with your friends, or when someone offers you a cigarette—and do it without shame.

It's almost impossible to trust yourself in the face of decisions when you lack confidence. You'll constantly seek validation from others and do things because *they* think it's a good idea. It's a recipe for personal frustration and disappointment. If you decide to do anything at all, you should do it because it's *your* choice, not because your friends are doing it, not because you're worried that *not* doing it will make you look bad, and not because it's expected of you. When you're confident, you know that every choice you make is your own and that it's good for *you*.

(Disclaimer: I'm not encouraging you to say no when your mom, dad, or guardian asks you to do your chores! That's different.)

Confidence helps you build authentic relationships

When you exude self-assurance, it creates a welcoming aura that makes others feel comfortable around you and opens up channels for clear communication, which can prevent misunderstandings and promote stronger connections.

Confidence also makes you assertive. You can stand up for yourself by drawing boundaries and communicating your needs clearly but respectfully. However, a relationship is a two-way street, so you need to be able to listen, too. Here, too, confidence saves the day, because you'll be less preoccupied with self-doubt and be able to really focus when someone else speaks. This makes you empathetic and a strong ally who your friends can rely on.

RECAP: WHY YOU SHOULD CARE ABOUT BEING CONFIDENT

Because when you're confident, you can
CONNECT with your true self and live life to the fullest.
Conquer fears and embrace opportunities.
Overcome challenges with resilience.
Navigate life's twists and turns with positivity.
Never make choices that don't feel right to you.
Elevate your outlook on life.
Communicate effectively for better relationships.
Trust yourself.

THE SCIENCE OF CONFIDENCE

No worries—we're not diving into boring formulas or undecipherable theories here. We'll just chat about some important stuff you need to know.

But . . . Why? Science sucks!

I know.

Yet beyond the classroom, science is fascinating. There are a ton of research topics, and while many of them are pretty meh, others are amazing, like the science of confidence, psychology, and how the brain works. They're super important fields because they help people understand themselves so much better. And, no, you don't need to become an expert to fully appreciate what your mind can do for you. Hopefully, this section will spark your interest in learning more about how your brain works from a psychological and neuroscientific point of view.

Still not impressed? OK, here's why it's in your best interest to learn about the science of confidence:

- **Awareness is a superpower:** Knowing more about how your brain works empowers you to take control of your life with confidence.
- **Break the myth of perfection:** Research shows that everyone struggles with self-doubt. Learning about it encourages you to accept your imperfections.
- **Rewire your brain:** Positive self-talk, stepping out of your comfort zone, and celebrating small successes actually work. Research supports their effectiveness.
- **Appreciate the chemistry of confidence:** A confident brain leads to happiness, motivation, and a positive outlook on life.
- **Adopt a growth mindset:** Understanding your mind's power and its ability to develop and adapt allows you to embrace a growth mindset and boost your confidence.

Without further ado, let's dive into some sciency goodness.

Epistemic confidence vs. social confidence

What is epistemic confidence?

This type of confidence has to do with how sure you feel about what you know. Here's an example:

> **You:** "Did you know the key to academic success is hard work and putting in regular study time?"
> **Me:** "Really? Are you sure?"
> **You:** "Yup. I've read up on it. Regular study habits improve your memory, understanding, and overall success in exams. And I've tested the theory . . . Since I've been at it more consistently, my grades have gone up."

Here's another example:

> **You:** "This game is terrible. The guy who made it didn't have good programming skills. You really need a decent understanding to make great games."
> **Me:** "Really? I heard it was easy . . ."
> **You:** "Why don't you program a game, then?"
> **Me:** "Uh . . ."
> **You:** "It's not easy. I've studied the field since forever. Trust me, without really good program-

ming skills, there's no way you can design top-notch games."

In both examples, you showed high epistemic confidence, or a solid belief in your knowledge, opinions, and conclusions. High epistemic confidence results from intense study of topics that you need to know (to graduate) and topics that interest you. This type of confidence allows you to feel sure of your knowledge and abilities and gives you trust in your own judgment.

However, a pitfall of epistemic confidence is developing a fixed mindset. Being too certain of your opinions can hinder personal growth. It's important to keep an open mind and be willing to adapt when necessary.

What is social confidence?

This is the one we all struggle with sometimes. Social confidence is about how sure you feel about yourself when dealing with other people. Let's see it in action:

> **You:** "Hey! Wanna hang out with some of my friends and me?"
> **Me:** "Mm . . . I'm actually an introvert, so . . ."
> **You:** "Perfect! It's not going to be a crowd or anything like that. We'll just chill."
> **Me:** "Oh, good! Let's do it, then."

And here's another example:

> **You:** "Hey! Wanna hang out with some of my friends and me?"
> **Me:** "Yes! I love meeting new people."

Would you be surprised if I told you that my character showed confidence in both examples? Parties are one of many social situations you'll find yourself in throughout life. But I used it as an example to make an important point: Being an introvert doesn't make you insecure. You *can* not like crowds and still be the person who oozes self-assurance. So, in the first example, my character only hesitated because she didn't like the idea of having to deal with lots of people, but the moment she realized it would be a small get-together, she was happy to go. (It's not that she couldn't handle a big crowd if she had to, she just has her preferences, and that's OK—we're all unique.)

So, social confidence helps you to relax in social settings and generally makes you more approachable and likable. Moreover, it helps you to listen to others, voice your own opinions, and build authentic relationships.

So, what's the difference, and is one more important than the other?

	EPISTEMIC CONFIDENCE	SOCIAL CONFIDENCE
What is it?	A strong belief in your knowledge, abilities, and opinions.	The ability to feel comfortable and be self-assured when you're interacting with other people.
Focus	Internal: It's about your personal certainty in what you know and that your ideas are worth exploring.	External: It's about building connections and being seen as a confident person by others.
Flexibility	Epistemic confidence can hinder your growth if it makes you resistant to others' opinions or new information that challenges your beliefs.	The antidote to too much epistemic confidence! Social confidence makes you willing to listen, be open to new ideas and experiences, and be adaptable.
Advantages	-Boosts your self-assurance. -Fights self-doubt. -Allows you to take action. -Gives you the boldness to stand up for yourself and defend your beliefs.	-Boosts your social skills. -Helps you build meaningful relationships and friendships. -Promotes a positive self-image.
Example	"I know my stuff!"	"Let me show you how and why I know my stuff, and then you can tell me about the stuff you know."
Is one more important or better than the other?	Nope. Epistemic and social confidence are soulmates. If one suffers, so does the other. Likewise, you can't thrive in one type of confidence without it affecting the other. The more you believe in yourself and what you know, the bigger urge you'll have to stand up for it. And the more comfortable you feel around other people and their opinions, the more you'll want to share what you know and believe.	

Neuroscience and confidence

While psychology helps us understand our behavior better, neuroscience (the study of the brain and nervous system) helps us understand the link between our behaviors and brains.

Can neuroscience help boost confidence?

You bet it can! Thanks to neuroscience, the myth that confidence is bestowed upon a select few at birth has been thoroughly debunked. While some people may be more predisposed to confidence, anyone can develop it. Let's look at how you can use neuroscience to boost your confidence:

Take control of how you respond when things go south

When faced with adversity, your brain releases stress hormones that can lower your confidence. However, when good things happen, your brain releases feel-good hormones that boost confidence. While you can't control every situation, you can control how you respond. By behaving in a way that promotes the release of feel-good hormones, you can prevent your confidence from plummeting.

I used to cringe at the thought of having to speak in front of people. Seriously, just thinking about it triggered nausea and made my palms clammy. Then I learned that hormones could influence confidence, so I decided to put it to the test.

My first mission was learning to speak confidently in front of just five people. With my goal set, the next challenge was to trick my brain into producing more feel-good hormones than stress hormones while I talked in front of people.

My solution? Stand-up comedy.

The first time I stood in front of the mirror to practice, I felt incredibly stupid. But I smiled, straightened my back, and told myself, "You're gonna ace this!"

Before I knew it, my best friend couldn't stop laughing at my jokes. I was dumbstruck but totally satisfied. One day, without even thinking about it, I was telling a joke to *seven* people.

Speaking in front of people still gets me nervous sometimes, but I never back away anymore; I don't get nauseous, and the icky palms are a thing of the past. And if my nerves get me worked up too much, I simply tell a joke to break the ice and get my feel-good hormones flowing.

Realize that your brain doesn't always get it right and remind it of your strengths and accomplishments.

Ever made a mistake that made you want to disappear? And then realized it wasn't that bad afterward? What's up with that?

Well, the human brain has a nasty habit. It does this annoying thing where it zooms in on moments of failure, embarrassment, and your weaknesses more than focusing on your strengths and triumphs. So, if you make a mistake, your brain kind of glitches and tells you that you're not good enough. The only reason you may believe this negative self-talk is that you have never questioned those thoughts. But by challenging negativity when it pops up, you can begin to change the way you respond and feel when slip-ups happen.

Build confidence by creating new beliefs about yourself

If you push yourself to participate in activities that require confidence, doubt yourself less, and start feeling comfortable around people, you can effectively change your self-image and what you believe about yourself.

If you currently believe you're not one for group activities, you'll experience stress at first. That's normal. But do your best to avoid coming up with "I can't do this" excuses. I promise, the first one will be the hardest. After that, you'll feel so much better and realize you're stronger than you thought.

Catch confidence from other people . . . Kind of like a cold, but with benefits!

Your brain and nervous system produce mirror neurons that fire up whenever you perform actions or watch others perform actions. This means that your brain can simulate what the other person is doing without you physically doing it yourself.

What does that mean?

Spending time with confident people allows their confidence to rub off on you because your mirror neurons internalize their words and behavior. It's like a contagious effect that influences you to think, talk, and behave more confidently. The best part is that you can catch the confidence bug whether you're physically present with confident people or watching them on a screen. Think about your favorite singer, athlete, or even a cool character from a movie. These role models exude confidence, and as you watch and learn from them, your mirror neurons go wild, allowing you to pick up their confident moves and mindsets.

Fun fact: You can spread confidence, too.

When you believe in yourself and show it to your friends, they can catch your confidence bug. By being self-assured, speaking up, and expressing your opinions, you automatically inspire others to do the same.

Here are some ways to catch and spread the confidence bug:

- Hang out with confident people.
- Emulate positive role models.
- Share and encourage confidence through your own actions.

RECAP: THE SCIENCE OF CONFIDENCE

- It's important to understand the science of confidence because if you know how your brain works, you can take control of your life.

- You get two types of confidence: epistemic and social. Both types are important for your personal growth. You can't have one without the other.
- Neuroscience proves that anyone can acquire and develop confidence.
- You can use your knowledge of neuroscience to boost your confidence. For example, you can use methods like learning to control how you respond to bad situations and changing your relationship with negative beliefs about yourself.
- Confidence is contagious—use it to your advantage!

THE CONFIDENCE-COMPETENCE LOOP

What is it?

Imagine a loop where confidence and competence are intertwined and constantly influencing each other. The cycle starts with the belief in yourself and your abilities (confidence) and propels you to develop the skills and knowledge to back up that belief (competence).

The more confident you are, the more motivated you become to take action and improve your skills. And as you gain competence in a particular area, your confidence grows even more, creating a positive feedback loop.

Think of it this way: Confidence is like the fuel that propels you forward, while competence is the engine that drives your progress.

Why you should care about the confidence-competence loop

A basic understanding of the loop can accelerate your journey of becoming confident in various aspects of your life:

- It will help you overcome fear and anxiety faster.
- It will help you set goals and reach them.
- It can help you enjoy the learning process and stay motivated.

RECAP: A LOOP FOR LIFE-LONG SUCCESS

Here's an easy way to remember what the confidence-competence loop is and how it works . . . Call it the CCC-Loop:

C > Confidence (believe in yourself and your abilities)

C > Competence (build your skills and knowledge)

C > Circle back! (gain even more confidence and reach your full potential!)

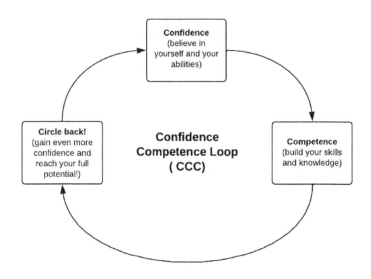

That's a wrap! Now that you know confidence is well within your reach, I bet there's *nothing* that can hold you back from getting it. And you know what? You deserve success, happiness, and an awesome life—so don't settle for anything less.

If you ever need a refresher on anything we talked about in this chapter, head over to the *Recap* part of each section.

In the next chapter, we're going to talk about where self-doubt comes from and, better yet, how you can overcome it. See you on the other side.

END-OF-CHAPTER ACTIVITY: FIND A GROUP ACTIVITY TO BOOST YOUR CONFIDENCE

In a notebook, write down a list of your interests and hobbies. Go through each one and think of ways you can pursue them in a group setting. For example, if your list contains "art," you can write "art workshops" or "art classes" next to it as possible activities. Or, if your list contains "reading," you can add "book club" as a possible activity. If you have "baseball," possible activities could be "ask friends to play for fun" or "try out for the baseball team."

When your list and possible activities are complete, draw a box or circle around your top five choices.

Before you make a final choice, chat about your interests and plans with your friends and family. Don't be shy to ask them what they think about it or even what they think would be a good fit for you. If you can, talk to people who are already doing those activities and ask them any questions that come to mind. It's possible that you'll scratch out one or two activities after your talks.

Take a day or two to think everything over. Imagine yourself participating confidently in each of the remaining activities on your list. Finally, choose the one that resonates with you most, take a deep breath, tell yourself you've got what it takes to do it well, and dive in!

CHAPTER 2
THE ROOTS OF SELF-DOUBT (EXPLORING SELF-DOUBT PART 1)

> *"I have self-doubt. I have insecurity. I have fear of failure. I have nights when I show up at the arena and I'm like 'My back hurts, my feet hurt, my knees hurt. I don't have it. I just want to chill.' We all have self-doubt. You don't deny it, but you also don't capitulate to it. You embrace it."*

> KOBE BRYANT

You have a friend, Aubrey, who's brilliant, full of positivity, and a bundle of energy whenever you guys are together. He always shares his ideas and dreams with you, but among other people, it's like Aubrey becomes a different person. He becomes quiet and hovers in the background while everyone else does the talking. It's weird because whenever someone mentions a topic you *know* Aubrey is passionate about, it's like he doesn't even care. And it doesn't happen among friends and classmates only—he has told you so many times that he wants to go traveling after he graduates and get away from the family business. But you've never heard him protest when his dad talks about the law schools he should aim to get into.

Now, I know you wouldn't be caught dead admitting it (and neither would your friends if they were reading this!), but I'm pretty sure you get how Aubrey feels. He has self-doubt, and it's making him question himself . . .

- *Am I good enough to voice my opinion?*
- *Does anyone even care about the things I care about?*
- *What if I make a fool of myself?*
- *I'm not even sure I want to study right after high school, but what if I disappoint my parents if I don't?*

At other times, the self-doubt gets a little mean . . .

- *You can't do it. Period.*
- *Not gonna happen . . . You're too much of a wimp.*
- *Don't even think about it! That kid is way better at this than you are.*

Self-doubt happens to all of us, and it doesn't matter how old you get, it's going to accompany you for the rest of your life.

OK. I know that sounds bleak but hear me out.

Self-doubt has its place. It draws the important line between arrogance and confidence. And, coupled with healthy doses of stress, self-doubt serves as a reminder that you are, in fact, just human.

In this chapter, we'll explore what self-doubt is, where it comes from, how it influences you, and how you can tell it to move over so you can be the one at the steering wheel of this thing called life.

WHAT IS SELF-DOUBT?

Self-doubt is that annoying, nagging, second-guessing gremlin sitting on your shoulder. It makes you question your abilities, potential, and worth. It's also the source of negative self-talk, which we'll explore in Chapter 6. Self-doubt can cause insecurity, which is the exact opposite of confidence. If you give in to self-doubt, you might end up thinking you're not as smart, talented, or capable as everyone else.

But here's the truth: Self-doubt is just a feeling. It doesn't define who you are or determine your potential.

Besides, how much power does a pesky little gremlin have if you can just flick it off your shoulder when it misbehaves? Granted, you can never get rid of it, but every time you flick it off, you'll send a clear message that *you're* in control. Eventually, that little gremlin will learn to behave (as best it can) and become quieter.

Self-doubt is normal and OK, as long as you don't allow it to stop you from growing, expanding your boundaries, and living life to the fullest.

And let's face it, arrogance is just a defense mechanism against feelings of intense insecurity. So, if you have to deal with an arrogant classmate, don't take them seriously. Just tell yourself that their gremlin is out of control and walk away. It's the bravest and most confident thing you can do—it proves your maturity and intolerance for gremlin behavior.

RECAP: SELF-DOUBT? OH, IT'S JUST A LITTLE GREMLIN . . .

Self-doubt is a feeling of uncertainty about your abilities that can destroy your confidence. Think of it as an annoying, nagging gremlin full of drama and negativity.

But remember, self-doubt can never define your worth. Flick that gremlin off, show it who's boss, and let your confidence shine!

UNMASKING THE GREMLIN: WHAT CAUSES SELF-DOUBT?

Comparisonitis: the social media trap

Ever stumbled upon a photo of a classmate on a sunny beach, their carefree smile making you question why your life isn't as glamorous? Welcome to "comparisonitis," where social media feeds self-doubt. In this era of carefully curated highlight reels, it's natural to compare yourself to others. But remember, those filtered posts only reveal a fraction of the story.

How comparisonitis affects your self-esteem

In social psychology, there's a term called "upward social comparison." It refers to when you compare yourself to someone you perceive as better. For instance, you might look at the star athlete in your class and wonder why you're struggling to keep up while they ace every game. It can make you feel inadequate, like you're not measuring up.

Then there's "downward social comparison." This is when you compare yourself to someone you think is worse off than you. It's like looking at someone who doesn't do great in a school subject and thinking, "Well, at least I'm not as bad as them." It offers temporary relief, but it doesn't address your own insecurities.

Research shows that low self-esteem leads to more upward comparisons, trapping you in a cycle of feeling worse. However, not everyone ends up feeling down. Some use comparisons as motivation for self-improvement. It all depends on your perception of control and your belief in the possibility of change.

For example, imagine you're aspiring to be a faster runner, and you often compare yourself to the best runner you know. But instead of feeling inadequate, you feel inspired to learn from their technique. At the end of the day, it's all about channeling the comparison into positive growth.

How to handle comparisonitis

Don't be fooled by what you see online—those are just the highlight reels. In the real world, we all face hardships and doubts—even if our profiles suggest otherwise.

Comparing yourself to those picture-perfect snapshots is like comparing an unfinished puzzle to a finished one . . . It's simply not fair! There's a whole struggle involved in adjusting and moving all the pieces before anyone gets to see that brilliant picture at the end.

Instead of falling into the comparisonitis trap, reframe your thinking. Embrace your uniqueness, talents, passions, and experiences. Your journey is yours alone, and that's something to celebrate. Life isn't a competition; it's about embracing growth, progress, and individuality.

So, the next time your pesky gremlin acts up, just tell it to shut up. Remind yourself that you're more than your online profile, and your classmates are more than theirs. Stop wasting energy on comparisons and redirect it toward self-acceptance, self-love, and celebrating your unique qualities.

Fear of failure: the "what if" game

There you are, minding your own business . . .

BAM!

An amazing idea pops into your head. It's the start of something huge, a dream waiting to burst into life. You can touch the excitement and passion bubbling inside you.

"But . . . What if everything goes horribly wrong and you fail?"

It's the self-doubt gremlin. Again.

Here's the thing about the gremlin: It's just trying to protect you. The human brain is wired to prioritize safety and comfort, so the fear of failure and the fear of the unknown often go hand in hand. There are times when the gremlin's response is actually valid. For example, if it warns you about not getting into a car with a random stranger, you should listen and get out of there.

But the gremlin has a problem—it can't tell the difference between danger and opportunity. It doesn't understand that playing it safe in every unfamiliar situation won't get you very far. Your job is to help the gremlin understand the difference.

Every successful person has faced failure at some point. Failure is as normal as breathing and should be viewed as a stepping stone toward growth and success. Just imagine if Thomas Edison had given up after his first few attempts at inventing the light bulb—we'd still be stumbling in the dark! He said:

> "I have not failed. I've just found 10,000 ways that won't work."

Instead of succumbing to the gremlin's "what ifs" and staying within your comfort zone, be bold. Challenge those doubts, explore your ideas, and pursue your dreams —even if it terrifies you. Take a deep breath, summon your courage, and make a promise to yourself that self-doubt won't control your destiny. Even if you stumble and fall, you'll learn invaluable lessons and uncover hidden strengths. Remember, failure is not the opposite of success; it's part of the journey.

In Chapter 3, we'll dive deeper into the anatomy of fear and talk about strategies to overcome it.

Negative influences: the dream snatchers

Picture this: You've overcome the fear of failure and now you're chasing your dreams like a boss. Next thing you know, you encounter someone who unintentionally blows a hole through your sails, forcing you to slow down or even halt.

Perhaps your friends question your abilities, or your parents express doubt about the feasibility of your dreams. It could also be the gremlin on your shoulder magnifying the doubts planted by others. Regardless, it feels like they're pelting little pebbles at your confidence, eroding it bit by bit.

Ouch, right?

Don't let them bring you down, though. We'll talk about how you can keep your head high in a bit, but first, let's talk about the two kinds of dream snatchers:

1. People with no interest in your success. They'll do and say anything to steer you off your course.
2. People who genuinely care about you but struggle to express their concerns in a supportive way.

Now, here's how to handle them: First and foremost, respect yourself enough to walk away from those who don't care. It may sound harsh, and it won't be easy, but it's the right and best decision. You'll never need the first type of dream snatcher. They'll only drain your positive energy and label you a coward. Let. Them. Go.

Surround yourself with positive, uplifting people who believe in you. This isn't about seeking validation or permission to pursue your dreams. It's about finding your tribe—the people who will cheer you on when you feel discouraged or distracted.

Dealing with the second type of dream snatcher is trickier, because they don't intend to put you down, and they honestly care about you. It's your responsibility to explain to them that their negativity isn't helpful. That said, remain open to their concerns and consider whether they might have a valid point. Perhaps their lack of support stems from how you're approaching your dreams rather than the dreams themselves. Just be willing to engage in conversations. Remember, confidence is not arrogance.

You're the captain of your own ship, sailing through the vast ocean of life. Stormy seas and rough waves may come your way, but you have the power to navigate your course. Never allow the dream snatchers to grab the steering wheel and change your trajectory. Take control, steer confidently, and sail toward your dreams with determination.

Past experiences

Negative past experiences are like tiny seeds of self-doubt. They take root in your mind and make you question your ability to succeed. It could be the memory of that test you studied hard for but didn't quite ace, the unintentional hurt you caused a friend, or the embarrassment and rejection you faced after pouring your heart into something.

Although it may not feel like it now, your past experiences don't have the power to define your future. They're simply part of the journey. Just because you faced setbacks in the past doesn't mean you're bound for failure. Remember what Thomas Edison said about finding 10,000 ways that didn't work? In your life, you'll encounter numerous paths that lead to dead ends, too, but that's just life. The trick is to persist and believe in yourself.

It's kind of like encountering a tough level in a video game: Every time you get knocked down, you don't give up, but you learn from your mistakes, adjust your strategy, and come back stronger every time until you push through. Every experience, good or bad, holds lessons and opportunities for growth. All you have to do is believe in your ability to learn and overcome any obstacle.

Embrace the ghosts of the past as friendly reminders of how far you've come and let them inspire you to keep pushing forward. You've got this!

Unrealistic expectations: the perfection trap

Setting unrealistic expectations for yourself is an open invitation for self-doubt. It can lead to disappointment and frustration.

The worst part about pursuing perfection? It's an illusion. It's like chasing the source of a rainbow. No matter how hard you try, you'll never attain that elusive state of flawlessness. And you know what? That's perfectly OK!

Who said life had to be flawless anyway? We're here to live, experience, and navigate through obstacles on our path to self-discovery. It's the detours and unexpected twists that give our lives meaning and provide unforgettable stories. Have you ever heard someone say, "Let me tell you about that time when everything in my life was perfect . . ."? It's unlikely, and even thinking about it might make you yawn with boredom.

Instead of fixating on perfection, shift your focus to progress. Life is a journey of growth, and every small step forward is worth celebrating. Whether it's acing a quiz, finishing a project, or mustering up the courage to try something new, every victory deserves recognition.

Stop setting unrealistic expectations for yourself and stop thinking your friends, parents, teachers, or mentors expect perfection from you. They don't. They only expect you to do your best—and there's a massive difference.

Give your all in everything you do and relish in the joy of progress. Nurture your skills, talents, and confidence. Yes, there will be setbacks and stumbles along the way, but keep going. With time and effort, you'll realize that realistic expectations mixed with mistakes are far more rewarding than unrealistic expectations that lead to nothing.

Embrace the messiness that comes with growth and aim to become the best version of yourself without striving for perfection—it doesn't exist!

RECAP: DODGE THE SELF-DOUBT TRIGGERS THAT FEED THE PESKY GREMLIN

Remember Professor Snape from Harry Potter?
Now there's a guy who could cause some serious self-doubt, right? Whenever you want to recall the causes of self-doubt, just think of Professor Snape:

S: Social media comparisonitis: the trap of comparing yourself to others.
N: Navigate the "what if" game by overcoming your fear of failure.
A: Avoid negative influences by dealing with dream snatchers.
P: Past experiences can never define your future.
E: Embrace realistic expectations and escape the perfection trap.

THE LINK BETWEEN YOUR EARLY CHILDHOOD EXPERIENCES, YOUR SELF-ESTEEM, AND YOUR CONFIDENCE

Think of your early childhood as the prologue to the epic tale of your life. How you were raised plays a significant role in shaping your confidence.

If you received love, support, and encouragement during your early years, it laid the foundation for a strong sense of self-worth and fortified you against self-doubt and insecurity. Conversely, if you had limited opportunities or a lack of support and encouragement, it likely made you more vulnerable to the self-doubt gremlin's influence—leading to lower self-esteem and confidence.

Just like tree seeds can germinate and take root wherever the wind blows them, we humans have no control over the circumstances we're born into. However, unlike trees, we have the incredible potential to make things work out in our favor, no matter what our early experiences were. You're the captain of your own ship, and you have the power to change course toward a life filled with high self-esteem and boundless confidence.

	SELF-ESTEEM	CONFIDENCE
Definition	It's equal to how much you value yourself as a person overall and determines how much you believe you're worthy of friendship, love, and recognition.	An unwavering self-belief in your abilities, potential, and social savviness (see epistemic and social confidence in Chapter 1).
Example	"I deserve respect and love because I'm pretty awesome in my own unique way!"	"I can totally do this thing!"
Relationship	Having high self-esteem can give you a boost of confidence in different areas. When you feel worthy, you're more likely to take risks and face challenges with a positive attitude.	If you lack confidence in something, it can chip away at your self-esteem. Doubts and negative thoughts can creep in, making you question your worth.
Interplay	When your self-esteem is low, it can be tough to build confidence. You might doubt yourself and feel unworthy of success. It's a real struggle.	At the same time, not having confidence in certain areas can bring down your self-esteem. It's like a cycle where one affects the other.
Importance	Self-esteem is like the foundation of how you see yourself as a whole. It affects your self-image, self-acceptance, and emotional well-being. It's a big deal!	Confidence is essential for taking action, going after goals, and overcoming challenges. It helps you grow personally and succeed in different areas of life.

Let's explore some practical tips that can help you change your course.

Reflect on your self-worth: Recognize your unique strengths, abilities, and potential. Celebrate your accomplishments, no matter how small, and remind yourself daily that you are enough and worthy.

Set achievable goals: If you have big dreams, good for you! But sometimes, a big dream can feel overwhelming and seem impossible to achieve. Break it down into smaller, manageable goals. Taking consistent action and making progress will cultivate a sense of accomplishment and boost your confidence.

Practice self-care and self-compassion: Prioritize activities that bring you joy, help you relax, and nourish your soul. Get enough exercise, sleep well, eat healthy foods, and feed your mind with good stuff. Practice positive self-talk and embrace your imperfections with compassion.

Explore your interests and develop your skills: Invest time in activities that ignite your passion. Whether it's a hobby, sport, art, music, or academic pursuit, focusing on something you love will provide a sense of purpose and contribute to your confidence.

Ask for support: Seeking help is not a sign of weakness but a courageous and wise choice. If you find it challenging to boost your self-esteem on your own, reach out to a trusted adult for guidance and support.

RECAP: WHERE YOU COME FROM DOESN'T DEFINE WHERE YOU'RE GOING
While your early childhood experiences may have influenced your self-esteem and confidence, you have control over how you develop them moving forward. Invest in your interests, set achievable goals, be mindful of self-doubt triggers, and don't hesitate to seek support from a trusted adult if needed.
You've got this!

END-OF-CHAPTER ACTIVITY: TAKE THE HELM, CAPTAIN!

In the above section, you learned about practical ways to change the course of your confidence-development journey. No matter the foundation you received during your early childhood, you'll always deal with people and situations that challenge your self-esteem and confidence. This activity will help you stay your course in the face of those challenges.

Ready? Grab a pen and notebook and let's do this.

Step 1: Highlight your strengths.
Think of three things about yourself that you're really good at or proud of. It could be anything from being an amazing friend, acing that one subject in school, or even that secret skill you use to impress people! Take a second to jot them down.

Step 2: Highlight your current challenges.
Write down the top three challenges you're facing right now. Maybe it's dealing with school stress, making new friends, or trying something you've never done before. Don't worry; we all have our share of things we have to deal with!

Step 3: Reframe your challenges.
This is the fun part. Imagine that those challenges are actually opportunities to show off your strengths. For example, if you're nervous about trying something new and one of your strengths is being an amazing friend, think about how you would encourage your friend to be brave.

Step 4: Visualize your confidence.
Imagine yourself as someone who has already conquered your self-doubt and visualize an outcome where you have overcome all three of your challenges. Can you feel the self-esteem and confidence emanating from you? Powerful stuff, right? It's totally within your reach.

Step 5: Take SMART steps to conquer all your challenges from now on.
Now that you know challenges are just opportunities in disguise and that it's possible to reframe them, that's exactly what you should do from now on. But don't just see the opportunity—set a SMART goal for yourself to conquer it:

Specific (clear and well defined)

Measurable (it should be easy to track from start to finish)

Achievable (realistic and attainable)

Relevant (align with your values and objectives)

Time-bound (have a deadline)

With this formula, you'll be truly in control of your life and be able to live with clarity, direction, and unshakable self-esteem and confidence.

Now that you understand the roots of self-doubt, it's time to dissect the biggest culprit behind it: fear. If you can, be sure to complete the above activity before you dive into Chapter 3.

Reminder: If you ever need a refresher on anything we talked about in this chapter, head over to the *Recap* part of each section.

See you on the other side!

CHAPTER 3
THE ANATOMY OF FEAR (EXPLORING SELF-DOUBT PART 2)

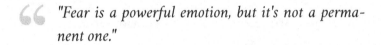 *"Fear is a powerful emotion, but it's not a permanent one."*

SUSAN JEFFERS

THE FUNDAMENTALS

Fear is your body's alarm system. Whenever you sense trouble or danger, it kicks in and tells you to do something about it. Imagine having to do something you hate. Whether it's giving a presentation, participating in a social or sports activity, or something your family expects you to do, your alarm system will typically kick in right before the event takes place. It will bombard you with a racing heart, shallow breathing, sweaty palms and armpits, and a barrage of "what if" thoughts. Then, just as you're about to take part in the activity, you'll have one of two reactions:

1. The "fight" response: You'll take a deep breath, try to calm yourself, and proceed with the activity, or
2. The "flight" response: You'll freeze, feel too overwhelmed, and not take part in the activity.

Conversely, there's anxiety—that nagging, uneasy feeling that makes you worry about things that may or may not happen. For example, before a big presentation, you might worry about tripping on stage, stumbling over your words, or making a blunder that will become the talk of the school.

While those are all possible scenarios, they're very unlikely to happen. And that's the thing about anxiety . . . ninety-nine times out of a hundred, people end up worrying about nothing because all the wild scenarios their minds imagine never happen. Even so, anxiety has the power to amplify fear like it's nobody's business.

Have a look at the table below to get a better idea of the difference between fear and anxiety, as well as the delicate interplay between the two:

	FEAR	ANXIETY	INTERPLAY
Definition	Your response to a specific and immediate threat or danger.	Your response to a vague and often imagined "what if" scenario.	Fear can trigger anxiety, while anxiety can amplify fear.
Examples	Being chased by a stray dog. Getting startled by a sudden loud noise. Fear of heights while standing in a tall building. Seeing the school bully approach you.	Feeling stressed over the upcoming exams. Worrying about social interactions and making friends (social anxiety). Racing thoughts and difficulty concentrating. Feeling restless and on the edge for no specific reason.	Your fear of failing an exam can trigger anxiety. Social anxiety can lead to the fear of being judged by others. Anxiety can cause an overall fear of losing control and a fear of failure.
How fear influences anxiety and vice versa	Fear can trigger a temporary anxiety response to prepare your body to fight or flee under normal circumstances. However, anxiety can make your fear reactions worse and make them more persistent and more intense. Left unchecked, anxiety can lower your threshold for fear responses, making everyday situations more threatening.		

HOW ANXIETY AFFECTS YOU

While anxiety is totally normal, it can interfere with your life if it gets out of control, so it's important to manage it. Training your mind to be calmer will make your responses to fear less severe and help you develop a higher fear threshold. This means you'll redefine what you perceive as threatening or dangerous (but don't do a Nala and go laughing in the face of really serious stuff, OK?).

Here's why you don't want anxiety to get out of control, like *ever* . . .

Anxiety can mess with your school life. When you're anxious, it's harder to concentrate, remember things, and make important choices. This can discourage you from doing schoolwork and make you avoid your education altogether.

Anxiety can mess with your social life, too. Worrying about being judged or rejected can make it hard to make friends, join group activities, and socialize. This, in turn, can make you feel isolated and increase your anxiety.

Anxiety can take you on an emotional ride, making you feel overwhelmed, angry, and frustrated. This heightened state makes it nearly impossible to relax and enjoy life because you're always on edge.

Anxiety can cause headaches, stomachaches, tense muscles, fatigue, and keep you up at night. As if that's not bad enough, it can weaken your immune system, making you more susceptible to illnesses or worsening existing health conditions.

Sometimes, when anxiety gets too overwhelming, it can **make people turn to dangerous "solutions."** Drugs and alcohol may seem like quick fixes, but in the long run, they can create worse problems.

Anxiety can strain family relations. It can lead to breakdowns in communication and cause conflict, confusion, and frustration for everyone.

If you don't address anxiety now, it can stalk you into adulthood and cause more problems. Living with unchecked anxiety can limit your personal growth, deprive you of opportunities, and make you unhappy.

Eventually, it can lead to more serious issues like depression or substance abuse.

UNDERSTANDING FEAR-BASED BEHAVIOR

How fear influences your behavior

Everyone knew Hannah as a fearless person. They looked up to her because she loved leading projects, speaking in front of others, and challenging her comfort zone. But she had a secret: She was afraid of water slides, and the mere thought of sliding down that colossal structure sent shivers down her spine.

One day, she had to face her fear while hanging out with her friends at the theme park. While everyone's laughter and excitement filled the air, Hannah's heart raced, and she felt an intense shortness of breath. Her self-doubt gremlin whispered in her ear, conjuring images of embarrassment, loss of control, and potential harm. It had a firm hold on her, suffocating her natural desire for fun and adventure.

Hannah watched as her friends soared down the water slide one by one, their cheers fading into the distance. The battle inside her intensified as the fear urged her to retreat and come up with excuses to avoid the challenge.

Hannah's fear of water slides may not be too serious, but let's examine the real issue: She knows everyone looks up to her because she's the brave one. So, maybe Hanna's deeper fear is losing her friends because they'll think she's a fraud when she doesn't take risks. And just because of that, she might go down the water slide. In this case, facing her fear would be a good thing, because she'll challenge her comfort zone and learn more about herself in a healthy way.

But what about next time?

How far would Hannah be willing to go to "prove" she's not a fraud? If, for example, her friends want to experiment with alcohol or drugs and she has no interest in doing so, will she cave in because she believes she's supposed to be the brave one?

Do you see how fear can influence your behavior? It can push you to take dangerous risks that compromise your values and well-being. In Chapter 7, we'll chat about how to overcome this kind of pressure.

Signs that fear is a hindrance in your life

Think of specific aspects of your life while reading through the below tell-tales. For example, you may think you're just determined to do your best in everything, but are you perhaps overdoing it in sports or academics to the extent that you're afraid of failing?

- You set impossible standards for yourself and feel like a failure when you don't reach them.
- You're settling for less than what you want in life.
- You say yes to things you should say no to, and vice versa.
- You have trouble speaking up and setting boundaries.
- You put things off until the last minute.
- You're a master at finding distractions to keep you busy so you can avoid projects and tasks.

The above behaviors are all associated with the most common worst fears teenagers deal with. We'll zoom in on those fears (and how to overcome them) in the 'How to overcome your worst fears' section.

How you react to fear and trauma

As a teen, you're not only dealing with fear, but you're also transitioning from childhood to adulthood. This is a particularly challenging time of your life, and sometimes you'll feel like things are out of control. That's normal. As long as you bounce back after setbacks and believe in yourself, you're doing just fine. Let's look at some ways you might react to fear and traumatic experiences:

- You'll experience an emotional roller coaster of sadness, anger, anxiety, and guilt, which can sometimes leave you feeling like you're stuck in a loop-de-loop.
- You may feel the urge to withdraw from family and friends when bad things happen. Taking some alone time can be helpful, but remember, reaching out for support is crucial too.
- Fear can make you react in unexpected ways such as acting out, rebelling, or giving up responsibilities. It's also possible to lose interest in things you used to enjoy. These are all part of your self-discovery journey. That said, if your acting out leads to trouble, or if nothing interests you for weeks or months, you should ask a trusted adult for help.
- Fear can make you pessimistic, cynical, and distrustful of others. It might even affect your memory, concentration, and problem-solving abilities. Don't worry, though—your mind is powerful and with time and support, you'll regain your mental ninja skills.

Remember, there is zero shame in telling your parents, a trusted teacher, or a mentor what you're going through. Even if you can't articulate it well, they'll feel honored that you went to them and will do their best to help you through your tough patch.

How to know when you're acting out of fear

- Pay attention to your body. It's like your personal fear-o-meter. If your heart starts racing, your palms get sweaty, or your stomach does somersaults, it's probably fear talking.
- If you catch yourself constantly doubting yourself or putting yourself down, fear is probably the culprit in your inner monologue.
- Are you avoiding situations or challenges because they make you feel uneasy? Fear often tells you to run and hide, but remember, facing them instead can lead to incredible personal growth.
- Trust your instincts. If something feels off, it could be fear warning you of real danger. Take a moment to pause, breathe, and listen to that gut feeling.

You've got the power to face your fears head-on and create a life filled with courage and resilience, but fear-based behavior can be a hurdle. Recognizing when you're acting out of fear is the first step to taking back control.

HOW TO OVERCOME YOUR WORST FEARS

This section may not address *all* the fears that are stealing your joy and holding you back, but it talks about the ones I'm almost 100% sure are gnawing at your confidence. I say "almost" because I'm not a mind reader (although my kids think I am sometimes!). It's just that I have a good idea because, through the ages, teenagers have struggled with a handful of common fears—myself, my siblings, all our old classmates, and your parents included.

If you can learn to overcome these common fears at this critical stage of your life, nothing will stand in your way.

THE FEAR OF NOT MEETING EXPECTATIONS

It feels like the entire world expects you to be a straight-A student, right? But, seriously, you're so much more than just your grades. This fear is linked to the pursuit of perfection. But you already know perfection is a game no one can win, so stop yourself before you get sucked into a frustrating cycle. Here are some practical tips:

Set realistic goals: Identify your areas of interest and focus on improving in those while maintaining a balanced approach to your other responsibilities.

Acknowledge your efforts: Even if outcomes don't match your expectations, take pride in your dedication and hard work.

Embrace mistakes as learning opportunities: Reframe your mistakes as valuable learning experiences. Analyze them, identify areas for improvement, and use them as stepping stones toward success.

Develop effective study habits: Create a structured study plan that allows you to manage your time efficiently. Break down large tasks into smaller, manageable steps, and prioritize your workload accordingly.

THE FEAR OF HOW OTHERS PERCEIVE YOU (SOCIAL ANXIETY)

We all want to fit in and have friends who appreciate us for who we are. But sometimes, our minds can create scary scenarios, telling us what other people must be thinking. It's like our brains are a little too creative for their own good.

Most of the time, though, the things you imagine aren't true. Trust me, people aren't sitting around judging you 24/7. They're too busy worrying about their own lives, what to wear tomorrow, or what's for lunch (or perhaps fighting their own social anxiety). Apply the following tips to overcome your social anxiety:

Embrace your uniqueness: Rock your quirks, talents, and your passions. Be proud of who you are and let that confidence shine through.

Start small: Social confidence doesn't happen in a snap. Begin by engaging in conversations with people you're comfortable with. Practice active listening, making eye contact, and asking questions.

Challenge your negative thoughts: Instead of assuming the worst, ask yourself, "What's the evidence for this thought? Is it really true?" Most fears are based on assumptions rather than facts. Replace those negative thoughts with positive ones, like "I am worthy of friendship," or "I have interesting things to say."

Practice, practice, practice: Like any skill, socializing takes practice. Join clubs or organizations or teams where you can meet people who share your interests. The more you interact with others, the more comfortable you'll become. Remember, it's okay to stumble or feel awkward at first. We all do!

Be kind to yourself: Don't beat yourself up if you feel nervous or make a social blunder. Remember that you're growing and learning, so treat yourself with kindness and compassion—just as you would a close friend who's going through a rough patch.

THE FEAR OF REJECTION

Rejection is a part of life. It happens to everyone, even the coolest, most popular people you know. But never forget: Opinions don't define worth. Here are some practical tips to beat the fear of rejection:

Embrace your inner bravery: Challenge yourself to do something that scares you a little every day—even if it's something small. The more you flex your brave muscles, the stronger they get.

Flip the script on rejection: Instead of viewing rejection as a personal blow, reframe it as a learning opportunity. Ask yourself, "What can I learn from this experience?" Maybe there's a fresh approach you can try next time. It's all about growth and resilience, and every rejection brings you closer to your goals.

Surround yourself with support: The friends you already have are your support squad. Share your goals and fears with them and let them cheer you on. They'll be there to lift you up when you're feeling down and remind you of your awesomeness.

Prepare for the possibilities: Before taking a chance, do a little homework. Whether it's asking someone out or going for an opportunity, gather some information and come up with a game plan. By preparing yourself, you'll boost your confidence and increase your chances of a positive outcome.

Be true to you: Never change who you are or what you believe in just to get someone's stamp of approval. Stay confident in who you are—the world will notice, and the right people will want to be your friends.

THE FEAR OF CRITICISM, THE FEAR OF GOSSIP, THE FEAR OF EMBARRASSMENT

THE FEAR OF CRITICISM

No matter how fantastic you are, there will always be critics out there. It's like they have a degree in nitpicking or something, right? Again, people's opinions don't define you. Here's what you can do to fight this fear:

Welcome constructive criticism: When someone offers feedback, take a deep breath, and listen with an open mind. Separate the helpful nuggets from the unnecessary negativity. Remember, even the most accomplished people have room for improvement.

Focus on self-acceptance: The most important opinion of you should come from . . . you! Recognize your strengths, celebrate your achievements, and learn from your mistakes. When you believe in yourself, the critics' voices are just faint blah-blah-blahs.

THE FEAR OF GOSSIP

Negative rumors are bad news for anyone's confidence. While there's no foolproof way to avoid it, you can definitely do a few things to overcome this fear while minimizing your chances of becoming the victim of gossip. Let's see what they are:

Mind your own business: Focus on being the best version of yourself instead of getting tangled up in other people's drama. Channel your energy into positive pursuits and let the gossip monkeys swing elsewhere.

Choose your tribe wisely: Surround yourself with friends who respect your boundaries and have your back. A good friend won't engage in gossip or spread rumors about you or others.

Lead by example: Instead of joining the rumor mill, lead with kindness and empathy. If someone tries to gossip in your presence, put your foot down and show that spreading positivity is way cooler than stirring up drama.

THE FEAR OF EMBARRASSMENT

Ah, the fear of becoming a walking, talking meme. Everyone has an awkward moment now and then. Ask your siblings or parents—it should be a fun conversation. Here's a story of what happened to me:

One day, I was visiting a friend's house, and her mom asked me what I was planning on majoring in when I went to college.

"I'd love to be an English major," I said, "but I'm not sure what career options are available for that."

My friend's mom replied, "Well, you could be a librarian!"

"Haha! Very funny . . . Who would do that?" I asked self-assured.

She just looked at me and said, "I'm a librarian."

Yep. I felt pretty humiliated. My friend's mom was a good sport and laughed it off and everything was fine, but I was incredibly embarrassed!

If (and when) something awkward happens to you, the key is basically going with the flow and not allowing that moment to haunt you forever. Here are some practical tips to overcome the fear of embarrassment:

Embrace your inner goofball: Life's too short to take everything seriously, so trip over your shoelaces and snort while laughing with pride. Remember, laughter is contagious, and being able to laugh at yourself is a gift that will serve you well for life.

Reframe embarrassment as growth: Every embarrassing moment is a chance to grow and learn. Instead of replaying the cringe-worthy scene in your head, ask yourself, "What can I take away from this? How can I handle a similar situation better next time?" Use these moments as stepping stones to become a more confident and resilient version of yourself.

THE FEAR OF THE UNKNOWN

Fear of the unknown is like standing at a crossroads and feeling uneasy about which path to take. It's natural to feel a little anxious or hesitant. Your brain likes to stick to what's familiar and predictable, and it will try to steer you away from the unknown without even considering that something incredibly exciting might be around the corner. Here's what you can do to feel less afraid of the unknown:

Embrace the thrill of the unexpected: Life would be pretty dull if we always knew what was coming next. So, shift your mindset from fear to excitement and let curiosity be your compass.

Expand your comfort zone with baby steps: Take small steps outside of what's familiar to make the unknown feel less terrifying. Maybe it's trying a new hobby, exploring a different genre of music, or joining a club or group that piques your interest.

Adopt the growth mindset: Whether or not your brain likes it, the unknown is where growth happens. Nurture the belief that you can develop your abilities through dedication and hard work and use challenges as opportunities. With a growth mindset, you'll always come out stronger and wiser (and have an epic story to tell).

Find comfort in the present moment: Often, the fear of the unknown stems from worrying about the future. Shift your attention to being present and making the most of each moment. When you're fully engaged in the present, the unknown becomes a little less daunting.

RECAP: CONQUER YOUR WORST FEARS LIKE A BOSS

Worried about not meeting expectations?

- Set realistic goals.
- Embrace mistakes.
- Develop good study habits.

Social anxiety bothering you?

- Remember, people aren't that focused on you because they've got their own stuff going on.
- Embrace your uniqueness.
- Challenge negative thoughts.
- Practice being social.
- Be kind to yourself.

Fear of rejection?

- Embrace bravery.
- Learn from rejections.
- Surround yourself with support.
- Stay true to yourself.

Afraid of criticism, gossip, and embarrassment?

- Embrace constructive criticism.
- Focus on self-acceptance.

- Mind your own business.
- Choose good friends.
- Lead by example.
- Embrace your inner goofball.
- Reframe embarrassment as growth.

Scared of the unknown?

- Embrace the thrill.
- Conquer your comfort zone with baby steps.
- Ask yourself: "Why not?"
- Embrace a growth mindset.
- Find comfort in the present.

THE CONNECTION BETWEEN FEAR AND SELF-DOUBT

John, the school's star tennis player, had a creative side that only his family, closest friends, and a trusted teacher at school knew about. The teacher convinced John that his classmates would be inspired to try new things if they knew about his passion. Eventually, John agreed to hold a solo art exhibition at the school's annual arts and crafts expo. He poured everything into creating his paintings and had immense fun doing it. However, as the expo date approached, he experienced a mix of emotions.

The night before the exhibition, John felt a sense of dread creeping in. He was worried about what his classmates might think of his art and whether they would appreciate his work. Fear made him anxious about receiving criticism and being rejected. He questioned his artistic abilities and talent, comparing himself to more established artists and telling himself he should rather stick to tennis. But soon after, he started doubting whether he was a good enough tennis player, too. He felt like a fraud.

Although distinct, fear and self-doubt often go hand in hand, and they can really interfere with your confidence and happiness. Let's see how they connect:

Fear can affect your self-belief: It can make you wonder if you're capable or good enough to handle challenges. The pesky gremlin may act up and say things like "You can't do this, you'll mess up!" The less you believe in yourself, the more these feelings can take over.

Self-doubt makes fear even scarier: When you already doubt yourself, fear can feel much worse. In turn, the fear intensifies your self-doubt and creates a vicious cycle that breaks down your self-esteem.

It makes dealing with life harder: When fear and self-doubt hit, you might try to avoid challenges altogether, procrastinate, or seek constant reassurance from others to feel better temporarily.

Excessive fear and self-doubt are both confidence killers and common obstacles to success in life, but both can be overcome with a positive mindset. Yes, developing a positive mindset is easier said than done, but with deliberate practice, the shift happens way faster than you think (we'll talk more about developing a better mindset in Chapters 4 and 5).

RECAP: WHAT'S THE CONNECTION BETWEEN FEAR AND SELF-DOUBT?

Fear and self-doubt sometimes team up to sabotage your confidence and happiness. Fear makes you doubt yourself, while self-doubt intensifies the fear. By cultivating a positive mindset, you can break this cycle and overcome these confidence killers, increasing your chances of success and happiness by a long shot.

END-OF-CHAPTER ACTIVITY: BEAT FEAR AND ANXIETY BEFORE THEY BEAT YOU

Step 1: Identify your fears and anxieties.
Take a few moments to reflect on your own fears and anxieties. Write down at least three specific fears or situations that make you anxious. These could be related to school, social interactions, personal goals, or anything else that comes to mind.

Step 2: Think about where they come from.
Try to identify the root cause behind the fears and anxieties you've listed. Are you afraid of failing or

being judged? Does the idea of rejection send chills down your spine? Or perhaps you hate thinking about the unknown . . .

Whatever it is, understanding why these things bother you so much may give you a whole new point of view. You may realize they're rooted in some simple incident that happened like forever ago. You may even discover you've been feeding yourself a bunch of lies over a TV series or movie you watched recently.

This step can help you see the truth behind a lot of things you think are real threats or issues. But if you don't feel better afterward, or if you managed to only get one or two fears out of the way, move on to the next step.

Step 3: Ask yourself: "What's the absolute worst that can happen if this fear comes true?"

So, maybe your fear has a REAL possibility of coming true. In that case, imagine for a moment that it does happen. One moment everything is fine and then suddenly that thing you've been dreading becomes reality. Your best friend has rejected you, the entire class is laughing at you, you weren't chosen for the team after all your hard work, or [think of your listed fears].

Now, ask yourself, "What's the worst thing that can happen now that my fear has come true?"

Jot down the possible outcomes.

If your best friend rejected you, some people may talk and stare. Maybe your ex-friend starts spreading rumors about you.

If you embarrassed yourself in front of the entire class, it may stick with you for a while. Bullies may make fun of you, or the story can spread like wildfire to the rest of the school.

Take a deep breath and take a good look at those possibilities. Let them sink in. Imagine it's as real as real can get.

Now, say this out loud: "I accept that these things can happen, and if they do, I'll survive. I'll be ready. But I'll never allow it to defeat me. Never."

You see, when you imagine the worst outcome and accept it in your mind before it even happens, something mind-blowing happens. First, the idea of it doesn't bother you as much anymore, and second, in the very, very, very (very!) rare case that it actually happens, it's not going to break your stride one bit. You'll hit the ground running from whatever height or angle you fall and simply move on with envy-worthy confidence.

BUT . . . this isn't the end of the story. You have the power to minimize the chances of worst-case scenarios to almost zero. Let's see how!

Step 4: Create a fear-busting action plan.
You know what you're afraid of and you know
where it comes from. Now it's time to (1) think
about what you can do to prevent it from happening, and (2) think about your game plan if it
happens.

Come up with a preventative plan:
There's no set-in-stone formula to follow because
each fear is unique. Your mission is to analyze each
fear on its own merits and then brainstorm ways to
prevent it from happening.

For example, if you fear being rejected by your best
friend, you probably need to have a heart-to-heart
in the mirror. Why would they reject you? Do they
expect you to do things you're not comfortable
with? Is your friendship dependent on you doing
these things? And if that's the case, are they really
your friend, or can you do better? On the other
hand, if you know your friendship is solid, then
maybe you should have a chat with your friend. Tell
them you have this crazy idea in your head that this
thing can happen, why you're afraid of it, and what
you think the consequences might be. Your friend
can probably do an excellent job at helping you put
this fear to rest.

Come up with an in-case-of-emergency game plan:
If your fear comes true, what are the next steps you'll take? For example, if you have a fear of embarrassing yourself in front of the class, think of ways you can turn the situation around in your favor if it should happen. Maybe you should be the one to make the first joke. Maybe train your mind not to react in a way that will make you look hurt and humiliated—if bullies can't see that they're hitting nerves, you take all their ammunition away.

Step 5: Immortalize your progress.
Keep a journal or a confidence diary where you record how you're overcoming your fears and anxieties. Write about your successes AND your setbacks, as well as the lessons you learn along the way. Finally, refer back to your entries often to remind yourself of your growth and resilience.

Now that you're armed with the knowledge of what self-doubt is, how it relates to fear, and know how to overcome it, you'll start spreading confidence vibes like never before.

But there's even more confidence to gain and more fun to be had! Head over to the next chapter to learn what self-awareness is, why it matters, and how to cultivate an unstoppable positive mindset.

THE POWER OF ONE VOICE

"When you have confidence, you can have a lot of fun. And when you have fun, you can do amazing things."

JOE NAMATH

Do you remember the story I told you in the introduction about the old man on the bench? I remember that moment years and years later, and the whole interaction couldn't have lasted longer than about five minutes.

A total stranger sharing his wisdom had that much impact on me. It's true that I had a lot to learn to gain that confidence he was talking about, but that one small conversation lodged in the back of my mind and boosted me on my journey toward finding it.

One voice can make a huge difference, and that's the reason I became a teacher. I knew I could help, and I've seen that to be true–not least as my students have grown in confidence. In fact, if I'm honest, it's in watching their confidence grow that I find the most satisfaction in knowing that I had an impact–more so than in the subject knowledge I teach.

But you don't need to be a teacher to make an impact in this way. Just a few sentences from you can have enormous power–just like those uttered by the man I met in the park.

You can help someone like you on their own journey to grow their confidence and settle into their true selves simply by pointing them in the direction of this book... and that can be done without even leaving the comfort of your own room.

By leaving a review of this book on Amazon, you'll show other young people that there's hope for them too, and you'll point them in the direction of the guidance that will help them become the confident person they long to be.

Simply by letting other readers know how this book has helped you and what they'll find inside, you'll not only show them that it's possible for them to grow their confidence; you'll lead them straight to the resource that will help them get there.

Thank you for your support. Every voice counts – including yours.

CHAPTER 4
BUILDING SELF-AWARENESS

> *"Look outside and you will see yourself. Look inside and you will find yourself."*

DREW GERALD

Dear Diary,

Today was mind-blowing! So, I met this boy named Bailey. There I was, minding my own business, when I saw him looking super depressed. I don't know what got into me, but I went up to him and asked if he needed company.

Listening to Bailey's story was like looking into a mirror! The stuff he shared was eerily similar to my own struggles, you know? But here's the crazy part: Just by being there for him, I discovered this hidden strength within myself—I'm actually a good listener. Who knew, right? And seeing Bailey's relief and gratitude was pretty awesome. Kindness goes such a long way . . . But I think it's about more than just helping others; it actually helps you learn about yourself.

Until next time!

WHAT IS SELF-AWARENESS?

Self-awareness means understanding your own actions, thoughts, and feelings really well. It's this amazing ability to look at yourself objectively and from a different perspective.

There are two types of self-awareness: One is about how you appear to others (public self-awareness), and the other is about understanding your inner thoughts and emotions (private self-awareness).

Being self-aware helps you in many ways, including:

- It gives you the power to influence outcomes in your life.
- You know what's right for you and make better decisions.
- You communicate with clarity and confidence.
- You have an open mind and understand different points of view.
- You act with fairness and understanding because you avoid making assumptions.

- You build better relationships because you can understand others' feelings better.
- You handle your emotions better.

Here's the cool part—self-awareness isn't some static thing we're all born with. As with building confidence, you can become more self-aware, and in this chapter, we'll chat about how you can build self-awareness and why it matters.

THE LINK BETWEEN SELF-AWARENESS AND CONFIDENCE

To really appreciate the link between self-awareness and confidence, let's revisit the definition of confidence:

> Confidence means believing in your abilities and embracing your individuality. When you're confident, you act on your beliefs and always push through when things get tough, no matter what. To build confidence, you need to practice a confident mindset every day (BEAPP up!).

Now, imagine not knowing yourself. You're not sure what you believe in, and you can't really pinpoint what you're good at. If confidence means believing in yourself and your abilities, but you don't know what they are, how can you become more confident?

That's where self-awareness comes in. It's the secret sauce you need to fuel your confidence.

Have you ever seen those incredible athletes who excel at their sport? They know their bodies inside out. They know their strengths, like lightning-fast speed or killer accuracy, but they also know their weaknesses, like maybe not being the tallest player on the field. With all that insider information, those athletes can play to their strengths and strategize around their limitations.

That's self-awareness in action!

It's like having your own user manual that gives you a rundown of your strengths, weaknesses, passions, and values. Not to mention the cool insights into what makes you tick, what makes you feel alive, and what makes you feel like you're in the zone. How could you *not* feel confident if you know so much about yourself?

And when you know yourself well, you naturally love yourself more—quirks and all. Ultimately, self-awareness turns you into a force to be reckoned with. You radiate confidence because you know who you are, what you stand for, and where you're headed.

How self-awareness builds confidence

When you know what you're good at and where you can improve, you can make smarter choices and set realistic goals for yourself. When you achieve them, you'll be rewarded with sweet confidence.

When you're self-aware, you're also more in tune with your values, passions, and beliefs. You know what truly matters to you, what sets your soul on fire, and what makes you unique. This deep understanding of yourself gives you a sense of purpose and direction, which makes you a more confident human.

Self-awareness is also about recognizing your quirks, insecurities, and areas where you can grow. We all have those, trust me! Being aware of your weaknesses puts you at an advantage because you can come up with strategies to overcome them and avoid awkward situations.

With self-awareness comes the power to say yes or no to new experiences on your own terms. You can make choices that align with your values and stay true to yourself, all while being mindful of how your decisions and actions impact those around you.

RECAP: WHAT IS SELF-AWARENESS AND WHY DOES IT MATTER?

Self-awareness means knowing yourself inside out. It's like having a mirror that shows you exactly who you are. Self-awareness matters because it's the secret to confidence, and you can't be a confident human if you don't know yourself.

SELF-REFLECTION AND MINDFULNESS: THE ULTIMATE MAP TO SELF-AWARENESS

What is self-reflection?

It's a fantastic, sunny day, and the math class is in high spirits. Rudy had just answered a question from the teacher, and now it's Callie's turn. She gets it wrong, but the teacher patiently explains the equation again and asks Callie to try again. Out of nowhere, Callie breaks down. She yells at the teacher, slams her book shut, and storms out of the class, leaving everyone perplexed.

Have you ever seen or experienced a similar situation? What happened to Callie isn't uncommon. In fact, even adults can have meltdowns like that. While the daily grind of life gets to all of us, there's something deeper going on here, and it has to do with how well Callie knows herself. She might think things over later and ask herself questions like:

- *Why did I react that way?*
- *What thoughts and emotions triggered my outburst?*
- *What could I have done differently?*

That's called self-reflection. Now, Callie may not have the answers right away, but this self-reflection is a very important first step toward building her self-awareness. If she does this regularly, she'll soon understand herself better and know why she does what she does, empowering herself to think things over before she has knee-jerk reactions in the future.

When you self-reflect, you explore the hidden layers of yourself that influence your choices and behaviors. It allows you to figure out what's going on inside your mind and heart. It's like being your own investigator, Sherlock Holmes style, but without the fancy hat and magnifying glass.

It's not always easy to self-reflect, though. We live in a crazy, fast-paced world filled with distractions like social media and Netflix. But carving out some quiet time for yourself, away from buzzing phones and binge-worthy shows, is totally worth it because self-reflection is a powerful tool for personal growth. It just helps you to respond better in tough situations.

Like, remember that time you got into a heated argument with your best friend? Well, self-reflection gives you the chance to think before you speak instead of blurting out hurtful words. It can help you make better choices and build healthier relationships.

Next time you find yourself in a sticky situation or feel confused about your emotions, try to self-reflect. It's like peeling back the layers of an onion (minus the tears, hopefully) and discovering the gem you truly are. Take a moment to pause, ask yourself some questions, and dig a little deeper. You might just find the clarity you've been searching for.

The benefits of self-reflection

You get to know yourself

Self-reflection helps you understand your core values, which are like your personal guiding principles. Knowing your values can make life's decisions a lot easier because you'll have a clear idea of what truly matters to you.

Discover your potential

Self-reflection is a powerful way of discovering your special talents and learning about your purpose in life so you can use it to make a positive impact on the world. It also gives you an opportunity to learn more about your strengths and weaknesses, which is pretty important for knowing where you rock and where you can improve.

Self-reflection makes you a big-picture thinker

Instead of getting caught up in the little things, you'll be able to see the grand scheme of things. It's like putting on a pair of special shades that allow you to see beyond the mundane and into the extraordinary. Seeing the big picture puts life in perspective and makes it easier to handle challenges, understand different viewpoints, and make better decisions.

Face your fears head-on

We all have things that scare us, but when you take time to reflect on your fears, you realize they're not as bad as they seem. It's like shining a flashlight on those dark corners and finding out there's nothing to be afraid of. Self-reflection makes you braver and more resilient.

Deeper connections

Self-reflection is great for building people skills. When you know yourself better, you tend to connect with people on a deeper level, have greater empathy, and can elicit a sense of appreciation for who you truly are. That's because most people simply gravitate toward authenticity.

Good vibes and good sleep

Self-reflection can help you keep your cool and handle tough situations without getting anxious or stressed out. Every time you self-reflect, you get a glimpse into what triggers your emotions, and you gain insights into how you can act differently if conflict arises or something potentially stressful happens. Your subconscious takes note of your discoveries and, when the time comes, it guides you to react calmly. And if you do some self-reflection before bedtime, it helps to clear your mind so you can enjoy a great night's rest.

Remember, self-reflection is not about being hard on yourself or getting stuck in a loop of self-criticism. It's about accepting and loving yourself—flaws and all. It's like giving yourself a big bear hug and saying, "Hey, I'm pretty fabulous just the way I am!"

RECAP: UNDERSTANDING SELF-REFLECTION

Self-reflection is like being your own detective, where you get to explore your thoughts and emotions to understand yourself better. It helps you make better choices, build healthier relationships, and unleash your potential. Above all, self-reflection is about accepting and loving everything that makes you you.

What is mindfulness?

Mindfulness is the ability to enter the ultimate state of chill by letting go and simply enjoying the present moment to the max. It's a moment of bliss where you release yourself from overthinking everything.

Here's the deal: We all tend to zone out and get lost in our own thoughts, right? It's totally normal, however, sometimes it makes us feel anxious and disconnected . . .

What about this thing?

What about that thing?

What if . . . ?

You know how it goes. Luckily, there's mindfulness. It's a super effective way to snap yourself back to reality so you stay cool and collected. You can try all sorts of different ways to practice mindfulness, like chill meditation sessions, taking mindful walks, or even combining it with activities you love, like yoga or sports.

Embracing mindfulness is like saying "peace out" to stress, and it comes with perks:

- You can boost your performance in all areas of life.
- You can become better at cultivating self-awareness and gain even deeper insights about yourself.
- And you can be more attuned to the well-being of your family, friends, and classmates.

But mindfulness isn't just about sitting cross-legged and chanting "om." It's an entire lifestyle. It's about being super aware of everything you do, from brushing your teeth to dealing with your annoying little brother or sister.

Why, you may ask, is mindfulness such a big deal? Let's find out.

The benefits of mindfulness

Stress-busting magic

Mindfulness is like a stress-repellent shield. It helps you feel more relaxed, even when things get intense. You'll learn to handle stress well and boost your overall well-being.

Happiness booster

Feeling down? Mindfulness can help turn that sinking feeling into bliss, like a happiness potion for your brain. Research shows that mindfulness can reduce anxiety and depression, improve your mood, and make you feel calmer and more clear-headed.

It activates your concentration

Do you ever find your mind wandering off like a mischievous cat? Well, mindfulness can tame it by strengthening your focus and attention skills. You'll become the envy of your classmates with your quick thinking (not to mention all the tests you'll ace).

Better emotional regulation

Mindfulness gives you the power to handle your emotions like a pro, leaving you feeling more balanced and in control.

Mind and body fitness

Mindfulness practice can help lower blood pressure, ease consistent pain, improve sleep quality, and even boost your immune system. Plus, mindful eating can help you make healthier food choices and maintain a healthy physique.

Self-discovery

Mindfulness helps you become more aware of yourself, your thoughts, and your feelings. You'll gain a deeper understanding of who you are and learn to love yourself just the way you are. You're amazing, remember that!

Brain flexibility

Mindfulness gives your brain some serious flexibility training, kind of like yoga for your mind. You'll become a master of adaptability, creative problem-solving, and making smart choices.

RECAP: UNDERSTANDING MINDFULNESS

Mindfulness is the ultimate state of chill that helps you stay present and stress-free. It's a skill you can develop through super easy techniques that enhance all areas of your life. A mindful life reduces stress, boosts happiness, improves focus, and enhances emotional control. It benefits your mind and body, fosters self-discovery, supercharges relationships, and trains your brain to be flexible.

Now that you've got the theory of self-awareness down, it's time to get practical. Head over to Chapter 5 to learn some fun techniques.

CHAPTER 5

FOOL-PROOF STRATEGIES FOR CULTIVATING SELF-AWARENESS

> "*Of course I talk to myself! Sometimes I need expert advice.*"
>
> ANONYMOUS

SELF-AWARENESS EXERCISES

Get curious about yourself

Cultivating self-awareness is like embarking on an epic journey of self-exploration. Picture your mind and heart as uncharted territory, just waiting for you to set foot on its unexplored paths.

Before you go to bed every night, take a moment to reflect on your thoughts, feelings, and actions of that day. The idea is to reflect, so don't get caught up in overanalyzing yourself or engaging in negative self-talk. Think of it as having a nonjudgmental conversation with a close friend and asking questions that can unlock the secrets of your inner world. Here are some ideas:

1. What were the highlights of my day? What made me feel happy, proud, or fulfilled?
2. Were there any challenges or setbacks I faced today? How did I handle them, and what can I learn from those experiences?
3. Did I show kindness or help someone today? How did it make me feel?
4. Did I engage in activities or hobbies that brought me joy or relaxation? How did they contribute to my overall well-being?
5. Did I manage my time effectively and prioritize my tasks? Were there any areas where I could improve my productivity?
6. Did I communicate and connect with my friends, family, or peers? Was I positive? Did I listen actively and express myself honestly?
7. Did I take care of my physical health today? Did I eat nutritious food, engage in physical activity, or get enough rest?
8. Did I learn something new today? What knowledge or skills did I gain?
9. Did I practice gratitude today? What am I grateful for in my life right now?

10. What could I have done differently today to make it better? How can I apply these insights to tomorrow?

Remember, self-discovery isn't a one-time event; it's a life-long quest. As you grow and navigate the twists and turns of life, stay curious and keep exploring your passions, strengths, and values. Be open to trying new things and learning from your experiences.

Accept your imperfections

Your flaws and quirks make you a one-of-a-kind and totally interesting person. So, cut yourself some slack. We all mess up sometimes. It's part of being human. Those slip-ups are stepping stones on your path to becoming more self-aware.

Remember that time you tripped over your own feet in front of your crush? Yeah, it was embarrassing, but here's the thing —it's not the end of the world! Instead of beating yourself up over it, try embracing the hilarity of the situation. Laugh it off! Believe me, a good laugh over your own blunders is excellent for your confidence. And hey, your crush might even find your ability to laugh at yourself super attractive.

Whether you're into comic books, love making terrible puns, or have an uncanny talent for mimicking animal sounds, that's what sets you apart from the crowd. Your quirks are the spice that makes life interesting, so own them with pride!

Now, let's talk about those tests that didn't go as planned. Trust me, even your parents have been there, too. It's easy to get down on yourself when you don't ace something you worked hard for. But success isn't linear and it's not about winning all the time. It's also about showing resilience and having true character when things don't go your way.

You know the saying about being a sore loser? Don't be one.

When you make a mistake or don't get the grade you wanted, take a deep breath and figure out what you can learn from the experience, and do it with a smile. Maybe you need to study more effectively, learn to ask for help sometimes, or simply give yourself a break when you're feeling overwhelmed. Embracing imperfection means accepting defeat and being open to improvement at the same time. That's how you discover your own unique strengths.

Take mirror time

This strategy isn't about perfecting your selfie game or practicing your smoldering gaze (although those can be fun, too). Instead, it's a me-time activity of getting to know yourself on a deeper level.

Here's how to do it:

Step 1: Choose a calm and private area where you feel comfortable and can have uninterrupted mirror time. Ensure you have access to a mirror or the front-view camera on your phone (preferably a mirror so your phone's notifications don't distract you!).

Step 2: Set a timer for five minutes and promise yourself you'll stay focused on the activity until the time runs out, and then settle into a relaxed and comfortable position in front of the mirror.

Step 3: Begin by observing the subtle nuances of your facial expressions. Notice the movements of your eyebrows, lips, and eyes. Pay attention to the emotions that arise and flicker across your face. See if you can spot the shifts in your facial features that reflect happiness, sadness, excitement, or other emotions. Stay present and allow yourself to experience and acknowledge these emotions without judgment. Reflect on the patterns you notice in your reactions, facial expressions, and body language. Are there certain triggers that consistently evoke specific emotions? Do you notice any habitual responses or gestures? Consider how these patterns might influence your daily experiences and interactions with others. Next, shift your focus to your body language. Observe how you hold yourself, the tension or relaxation in your muscles, and any gestures you make.

Step 4: When the five minutes are over, reflect on significant insights or realizations that emerged during the activity (better yet, write these reflections somewhere). Consider how this newfound self-awareness can empower you to navigate life and set an intention to carry your newfound self-awareness into your daily life.

Why does this activity matter, you ask?

Mirror time is an opportunity to deepen your connection with yourself. Accept the vulnerability and messiness of being human. Embrace the idea that you are worth your own time, attention, and love. By observing your reactions and emotions, you become more attuned to your inner state. You can recognize patterns and understand what makes you tick. It's like unlocking a treasure trove of self-knowledge.

When you know what triggers certain emotions or how your body language reflects your mood, you become a master of your own destiny. You're no longer at the mercy of random emotions or those knee-jerk reactions and can face life with intention and grace.

Mirror time may sound weird, but it works. The more you connect with yourself, the more you'll understand the reasons behind your behavior, feel empowered to change the things you don't like about yourself, and embrace the beautiful messiness of being human.

Journal your journey

You'd be surprised at what happens when you put pen to paper (or fingers to keyboard). Jotting down your emotions and thoughts can bring so much clarity and insight. It allows you to notice patterns, triggers, and the things that make your heart sing or your blood boil. It's like shining a spotlight on your inner world and saying, "Hey, I see you, emotions, and I'm ready to understand you better!"

Whether you find yourself in a tricky situation or are facing a mental mountain you need to conquer, your journal can be a trusted confidant. Not only does journaling give you a place to pour out your heart, but it serves as your personal time machine. Seriously, when you look back at your previous entries, you'll see just how much you've grown and evolved despite the obstacles.

Journaling isn't just about capturing the tough stuff, though. It's also a place to celebrate the little triumphs, the joyful moments, and the beauty of everyday life. Write about the things that light you up, the dreams you're chasing, and the experiences that make your heart do a happy dance.

Your journal is your sacred space to unravel the mysteries of your mind and heart, so let your thoughts dance across those pages. Explore your inner landscape, discover your strengths, and embrace your vulnerabilities. It's a great tool for self-awareness, growth, and self-acceptance. Above all, remember that journaling is a personal journey. There are no rules or judgments—it's just you and the blank pages waiting to be filled.

Hang out with real people

Personal feedback only goes so far, so spending time with real people in your quest to understand yourself better is pretty important. And, no, digital interactions alone won't cut it. Spending too much time online can eventually make you feel disconnected from the real world and make you miss out on little but important things happening around you, like the joy of a good hug or the pleasure of a shared joke. Besides, you won't know if there's a secret standup comedian or motivational guru living inside you if you don't mingle face-to-face.

When you engage with others in person, you get to share authentic experiences, have deep conversations, and truly listen to what others have to say. There's something special about being able to see someone's facial expressions, hear the tone of their voice, and feel their energy. It adds a whole extra layer of connection that emojis and GIFs just can't replicate.

When you hang out with people, their feedback can help you gain insights and perspectives about yourself. They can reveal things you might not have discovered on your own. Plus, nothing compares to heartfelt moments with your tribe. Those are the memories you'll cherish and the stories you'll be telling your grandkids someday (or maybe your holographic AI assistant in the future, who knows?).

Step away from the virtual world every once in a while and immerse yourself in the richness of human connection. The magic of real-life connections is something you don't want to miss out on.

MINDFULNESS EXERCISES

Mindful breathing

Find a cozy spot where you can relax with zero interruptions for at least five minutes. Maybe it's your favorite corner in your room or that oh-so-comfy bean bag chair. Now, close your eyes and take a moment to settle in. Focus on your breath—that magical rhythm of life flowing in and out of you. Notice the air as it enters your nostrils, maybe even feel how it tickles your nose hairs.

Breathe in . . . 1 . . . 2 . . . 3.

Let the air fill your lungs, like you're taking in all the good vibes of the universe.

Breathe out . . . 1 . . . 2 . . . 3.

As you exhale, let go of any muscle tension or mental stress. Feel the calmness washing over you like a wave gently caressing the shore.

Keep focusing on your breath.

Inhale and imagine all the positivity and confidence entering your body.

Exhale and let go of any doubts or negativity that might be holding you back.

Mindful breathing gives your brain a super relaxing spa treatment, pampering it with peaceful thoughts and tranquility. You'll notice the stress melting away, leaving you feeling refreshed and grounded.

Remember, mindfulness is all about being fully present in the moment. So, whenever you feel overwhelmed or need a confidence boost, pause what you're doing and take five minutes to tune in to your breath. It's like pressing the reset button and giving yourself the space to recharge and embrace your inner strength.

Even if you're in the middle of something and can't get away, you can use this exercise to calm your nerves right there and then. Trust me, it's that powerful! Focus on your breath with deep inhales and exhales until all your concentration shifts to your breathing, then ease back into the task at hand with renewed focus.

Mindful munching

It's time to take your snacking game to a whole new level. So, grab a tasty treat, whether it's a juicy piece of fruit or a scrumptious health cracker, and let's dive in!

Find a cozy spot in your kitchen (or wherever you feel most comfortable). Before you indulge, take a good look at your snack. Push all the thoughts out of your mind until your only concern is that yummy thing in your hand. Notice its colors, its shape, and how it's calling out to your taste buds.

Bring the snack closer to your nose and inhale deeply. Can you smell that mouthwatering aroma? Let the scents awaken your senses and build up the anticipation. It's like a prelude to the flavor symphony about to unfold!

Finally, take that first glorious bite.

But wait! Don't rush.

Take your time to feel the snack's texture against your lips and tongue. Is it smooth, crunchy, or perhaps a bit of both? As you chew, pay attention to how it feels in your mouth. Is it soft and juicy, or does it have a satisfying crunch? Notice the flavors as they activate your taste buds. Sweet, tangy, savory, or a delightful combination of them all? Let each bite be a moment of pure culinary bliss.

Chew slowly. Feel the food nourishing your body. Be fully present in this moment, free from all distractions. Relish the deliciousness. Immerse yourself in the experience with each bite. Notice how the flavors evolve and how your enjoyment deepens.

Mindful munching is not just about feeding your body. It's about feeding your soul. It's about celebrating the simple pleasures of life, even if it's just a snack in your kitchen. Take a moment to appreciate the experience and nourishment you've given your body. You've just transformed snacking into an art form!

Walk the zen way

Although you'll be moving for this exercise, the workout is more about your mind than your body, so take a slow(ish) stroll for at least 15 minutes and tune in to the present moment. Notice the sensation of the ground beneath your feet, whether it's the softness of grass, the pavement beneath your soles, or the crunch of leaves (you'll get a good sense of it even if you're wearing shoes). Treat each step like a gentle reminder to stay grounded and connected to the here and now.

As you move forward, broaden your senses from the ground beneath you to the world around you. Listen to the symphony of nature—the rustle of leaves in the breeze, the chirping of birds, or the distant hum of traffic. Let these sounds become the soundtrack of your journey, but don't let your thoughts wander—just focus on the sights, smells, and sounds around you. Notice the intricate details of the vibrant colors of flowers, the patterns on the bark of trees, graffiti on walls, or the way sunlight dances on and through various surfaces. It's like discovering a whole new universe right in your neighborhood!

Enjoy each moment of your walk with complete awareness. Feel the gentle breeze on your skin, savor the fresh air filling your lungs, and take in the scents of nature. Let it awaken your senses and remind you of the beauty that surrounds you. And hey, keep those eyes peeled for any unexpected surprises. Who knows, you might spot a squirrel doing a funky dance or a butterfly gracefully fluttering by.

Walking can be so much more than getting from point A to point B. It's a chance to embrace the world around you, be fully present in each step, and discover the beauty in ordinary things. As you reach the end of your walk, take a moment to appreciate the tranquility and sense of peace you've cultivated in so little time.

Puzzle time

Engaging in puzzles is not only a fun pastime but also an excellent mindful workout for your brain. Whether it's a word search, Sudoku, a brain teaser, or an old-fashioned jigsaw puzzle, they require focus, attention to detail, and problem-solving skills. By immersing yourself in the puzzle-solving process, you can experience a heightened state of concentration and mental clarity.

Appreciate the intricacies of each clue or puzzle piece. Notice how your mind becomes sharp and focused as you analyze the information and consider possible solutions. You know that feeling when you're fully immersed in something and everything just clicks? That's called the state of flow. It's super satisfying and easy to achieve when doing puzzles.

Sometimes, it can be difficult to immerse yourself in a puzzle from the get-go because of distracting thoughts. If that happens, sit back, and do the mindful breathing exercise. Once you're solely focused on your breathing, switch over to the puzzle and let all that focused energy flow into solving it.

Puzzle time is also the perfect opportunity to challenge yourself in a controlled and enjoyable manner. Each puzzle presents a unique set of problems to solve, and with each solved clue or completed puzzle, you experience a sense of accomplishment. This feeling of success and mastery can boost your confidence and self-esteem, reinforcing the belief in your abilities to overcome challenges. Beyond the immediate enjoyment and sense of accomplishment, engaging in puzzle time regularly can have long-term benefits for your cognitive abilities. By consistently exercising those cognitive skills, you can improve your mental agility, creativity, and critical thinking abilities.

Tech detox dance party

Technology has a nasty way of taking over every aspect of life. How many times have you grabbed your phone to record something epic instead of just absorbing the moment? It's not an accusation—I can't even keep track of how many times I've done it. And when I'm not careful, I find myself glued to my phone or tablet while hundreds of posts compete for my already divided attention.

The tech detox dance party offers a refreshing break from technology overload and an opportunity to let go and just enjoy the moment.

Dancing is a form of self-expression and a powerful way to connect with your body and emotions. As you surrender to the music, you release pent-up stress and tension. The physicality of dancing stimulates the release of endorphins (your natural happy hormones) and promotes a sense of ultimate well-being. It's like a burst of positive energy surging through your veins that releases you from the worries and stresses of life so you can reconnect with joy and playfulness. As you crank up the tunes, let the rhythm guide your movements. Dance like nobody's watching (because they're not, you know?).

This is your moment to let go of self-consciousness and fully enjoy yourself. Move freely and forget about judgments and expectations. Feel the music pulsating through your body as it ignites your energy and sets your spirit free.

END-OF-CHAPTER ACTIVITY: JUST DO IT, 'CAUSE THERE'S NO TIME LIKE NOW

Choose any technique from this chapter to do right now.

Before you start, grab a notepad and pen, and answer the following questions:

1. What is my current level of stress or anxiety on a scale of 1 to 10?
2. How would I describe my overall mood and emotional state right now?
3. How am I feeling physically?
4. How present am I at this moment? Am I fully aware of my surroundings?
5. What is one intention or goal I have for this practice? What do I hope to gain or experience?

When you're done, answer the following questions:

1. What is my current level of stress or anxiety on a scale of 1 to 10 compared to before the exercise?
2. How would I describe my overall mood and emotional state now? Has it shifted in any way?
3. How does my body feel now?
4. How present and aware was I during the exercise? Did my mind wander frequently, or was I able to maintain focus?

5. Did the exercise meet my expectations or intentions? In what ways did it positively impact me?

That's it—you're now a self-awareness guru in your own right!

But remember, self-awareness doesn't just happen. Like any relationship with a friend, you'll have to spend quality time with yourself if you want it to work, so come back to the exercises in this chapter often.

Don't forget, if you ever need a refresher on the ins and outs of self-awareness, flip back to the *Recap* section of this chapter.

Now it's time to expand your confidence into the exciting realm of positive self-talk.

Ready? See you in Chapter 6.

CHAPTER 6
CULTIVATING POSITIVE SELF-TALK LIKE A BOSS

66 *"Self-talk reflects your innermost feelings."*

DR. ASA DON BROWN

WHAT IS POSITIVE SELF-TALK?

Self-talk is like having a little commentator inside your head, chatting away all day long. It's your internal dialogue, consisting of a mix of your thoughts, beliefs, questions, and ideas. The way you talk to yourself is a powerful force that can impact how you feel and what you do.

When self-talk is positive, it's like having your own cheerleader or team of supporters, motivating you and boosting your confidence. Thinking positively about yourself results in you feeling oh-so-good and optimistic. It improves your self-esteem, helps you manage stress, and makes you more resilient in the face of challenges. When self-talk turns nasty, though, it becomes an annoying little voice that brings you down and makes you doubt yourself. This is called negative self-talk, and it's a real buzzkill. It's like a cloud of doubt that doesn't reflect reality but still makes you feel like you're going to fail even before you start.

The most important thing to know about self-talk is that you *always* have the power to make that voice more positive and supportive. We'll dive much deeper into this topic in the rest of the chapter, but for now, here are some cool tips that will help you conquer negative self-talk:

- Practice self-awareness.
- Recognize those negative thoughts the moment they appear and question if they're true or just exaggerations.
- Put things into perspective. Ask yourself if what you're worrying about will even matter in a few days, weeks, months, or years.
- Stop the thought. Visualize a stop sign or have your own little ritual to interrupt those negative thoughts. No one's watching!
- Replace the thought. Swap that negativity with kindness and encouragement.

Changing self-talk is like building a new habit; it takes time and effort. But you've got this, and together with the other techniques you've already learned, it will be your ultimate confidence-boosting weapon to rock at life!

RECAP: WHAT IS POSITIVE SELF-TALK?

It's all about being your own biggest fan with internal words of praise, motivation, and encouragement. And, yes, you can totally talk to yourself out loud. Adults do it all the time!

BEWARE OF NEGATIVE SELF-TALK

Josh was the school's best storyteller—hands-down. Everyone believed he had a bright future that involved becoming a famous author or screenwriter. While he knew he had talent and appreciated everyone's enthusiasm, Josh had a dark companion that never left his side . . . his inner critic.

Every time he sat down to write, that inner critic would rear its ugly head and bombard him with endless negativity.

"You're not good enough," it would say, *"your writing is terrible, no one will ever read it."*

These thoughts took root in Josh's mind, and he began to doubt his abilities and question whether pursuing his dream of writing was worth it. Sadly, Josh never learned to challenge his negative self-talk. He let it consume him, and eventually, he stopped writing altogether. He never shared his stories with anyone, and the world never got to experience the magic of his words. His fear of failure and lack of confidence in his abilities kept him stuck in a cycle of self-doubt and inaction. Over time, Josh's passion for storytelling dwindled, and he settled for a more conventional career path that felt safer—but it left him unfulfilled. He looked back on his school days and wondered what could have been if he had only found the courage to ignore his inner critic and pursue his dream.

Negative self-talk doesn't just get you down the moment it happens. As you can see from Josh's story, it comes with serious consequences if you fail to take control and turn it into positive self-talk. Let's have a closer look at what these consequences are.

Lack of confidence

You can follow every strategy in this book to build your confidence, but if you talk yourself down all the time, they'll mean nothing. That's because when negative self-talk takes over, you can't see your true potential anymore. Self-doubt will reign in your mind and your confidence will remain very low. Imagine feeling like you're not good enough all the time. No fun, right? It's *that* important to kick negative self-talk to the curb.

Decreased motivation and feeling helpless

Negative self-talk can drain your motivation like a leaky bucket. This lack of motivation will soon leave you feeling out of control and like you have no direction whatsoever. We call that feeling helplessness, and it can mess with your entire life on so many levels.

Increased anxiety and heightened stress

Negative self-talk can leave you feeling like you're carrying a heavy burden every day. It can also create problems out of thin air, leading to more stress and anxiety. Your mind will play tricks on you and make you believe almost any worst-case scenario it imagines. This constant worry and anxiety can be overwhelming and exhausting, and the worst part (or best part—depending on your point of view!) is that most worries never, ever come true.

> " *"Ninety-eight percent of the things we worry about never happen."*

> DALE CARNEGIE, *HOW TO STOP WORRYING AND START LIVING*

It can silence your voice and send you into hiding

You are destined for greatness. Your thoughts and ideas matter. But you can jinx yourself into the abyss of mediocracy if you give in to negative self-talk. It can force you to dim your light and hide your true self from the world. The truth is, you have so much to give, and your thoughts and opinions deserve to be heard—it's the only way you can make the world a better place. Don't allow negative thoughts to keep you from sharing your awesomeness with others!

Predictability and boredom

When you default to negative thoughts, your MO is to play it safe and stay in your comfort zone. It's like being stuck in a bubble where everything is predictable. Sure, predictability feels safe, but it's also boring. Life is meant to be exciting and full of adventures, and you deserve to experience all the amazing things it has to offer.

Limited thinking and missed opportunities

Negative self-talk clouds your vision and puts limits on what you believe you can achieve. It's like building invisible walls around your potential that prevent you from seeing the possibilities right in front of you. Opportunities often present themselves disguised as challenges, and you want to be able to recognize them. You can't do that if you're busy dissing yourself all the time. Remember that your thoughts shape your reality, so you owe it to yourself to create a supportive and positive internal dialogue.

Relationship issues and lack of connection with others

Speaking of walls, negative self-talk can make you put them up around your heart and avoid being vulnerable with others. It can also make you feel insecure and needy in close relationships. Meaningful relationships thrive on openness and trust, and as a social being, you really do need people if you're going to live life to the fullest.

Some serious regrets at the end of your life

Imagine this: You've lived your life and now you're old. Looking back, all you can see are missed opportunities, dreams left unfulfilled, and adventures never taken. Ouch.

As a teen, you have your whole life ahead of you, and it's filled with countless possibilities and opportunities. Don't entertain negative self-talk. If you do, it will convince you that you're incapable of achieving success and leave you feeling like you don't deserve happiness. You'll find yourself looking back with endless regret, wondering what could have been.

RECAP: NEGATIVE SELF-TALK IS A TOTAL KILLJOY

It saps your confidence, kills motivation, and fuels anxiety. It silences your voice, limits your thinking, and can leave you with regrets. Don't let it hold you back from living your best life and pursuing your dreams . . . Kick negative self-talk to the curb and embrace a positive, empowered mindset. You've got this!

Phew! With all that negativity out of the way, let's see what you have to gain from the opposite of the coin.

THE BENEFITS OF POSITIVE SELF-TALK

Let's see how Josh's life could have turned out if he had learned to beat his negative self-talk.

Maybe his dad realized what was happening and took it upon himself to help Josh.

As he watched his son struggle, Josh's dad didn't want him to experience the same regrets and unfulfilled dreams he had faced in his own life. He knew the answer was for Josh to challenge his negative self-talk. So, he decided to become Josh's mentor and biggest cheerleader. He encouraged him to share his stories with him and the rest of the family. Whenever the young writer faced self-doubt, his dad was there to remind him of his incredible talent and the positive impact his stories made.

Together, they learned techniques to challenge negative thoughts. They gave Josh's inner critic a funny nickname —Mr. Gloomy Grouch—and turned it into a playful game to disarm its power. Josh's dad reassured him constantly that negative self-talk was normal but conquerable.

With his dad's support and guidance, Josh began to see his writing in a new light. He realized that he was genuinely capable of pursuing his dreams. Every time the negative self-talk crept in, Josh turned it into positivity that motivated him to push through. His confidence grew and his writing flourished.

Years later, as Josh stood on a stage, accepting an award for his bestselling novel, he couldn't help but feel grateful for his dad's intervention. He knew that without it, he might have succumbed to his inner critic and never pursued his writing dreams. But he also knew that if he wasn't a fighter who could learn to believe in himself, his dad's efforts wouldn't have worked.

See how life can turn out radically different depending on how you talk to yourself? The question is, what kind of life do *you* want to live?

It doesn't matter what challenges get thrown your way, you always have the choice to (1) let it defeat you, or (2) let it be an invitation for growth and success. Which one you choose will depend a lot on your mindset, and your mindset depends on how you talk to yourself. Let's explore some benefits you can gain from cultivating positive self-talk.

Improved self-esteem

You're truly amazing and engaging in positive self-talk will ensure you never forget it. When you fill your mind with encouraging words and thoughts, your self-esteem gets a mega boost. You'll walk with your head held high, knowing that you're a superstar in your own right. So, take a good look at yourself in the mirror and embrace thoughts like "You're capable" and "You're worthy."

Healthier immune system and increased vitality

Positive thoughts encourage your body to release happy chemicals that boost your immune system, kind of like a secret health-boosting potion. This means your body will be on alert and ready to fight whenever bugs try to invade and mess with you.

Positive self-talk also works its magic in your body's energy department. It pumps you full of life and vitality so you can make the most of every moment.

Less Pain

Who knew thoughts could have a say in how much something hurts? It's true! Positive self-talk is like a soothing balm for your brain. It sends calming signals to your nervous system, telling it to turn down the pain volume. When you have to face a needle at the doctor's office or deal with a sore muscle after a workout, remember to be kind to yourself. Say things like "You're strong; you can totally handle this," and watch how it eases the ache.

Your heart will thank you

When you think positively, your heart feels lighter and happier, just like when you hear your favorite jam. A happy heart is a healthy heart. By keeping yourself busy with uplifting thoughts instead of negative ones, you're helping your heart to stay in tip-top shape.

A strong mind

By now, you've learned that life can be a wild ride. Positive self-talk is like a safety harness that protects your mental health on really bad days. When you talk kindly to yourself, you build resilience. Think of it as a mental muscle that helps you to stay confident and ready to bounce back from tough times.

Less stress

You know those negative thoughts that try to make you worry and freak out that we talked about earlier? They've got nothing on your positive self-talk shield. Positive thoughts will always help you see a way out, and even if things go wrong, you'll know it's not the end of the world. Besides, when you're more focused on how well you're handling life, there's really no time for worrying.

Killer coping skills

Engaging in positive self-talk doesn't mean trying to ignore the fact that life can be hard to deal with. Setbacks will happen (a lot), but positive self-talk is the umbrella that keeps you dry in the storm. It helps you find the strength to handle tough times, learn from them, and grow into a strong person and a role model of resilience to others.

Better relationships and stronger connections with others

Positive self-talk helps you build a strong foundation of self-love and kindness. When you treat yourself with respect, that good energy radiates to others, too. You're more open to forming connections and this allows you to become a better friend, sibling, or boyfriend/girlfriend because you know how to uplift and support others.

Superhuman focus

Got a goal in mind? Positive self-talk helps you lock onto that target like a laser beam. When your thoughts are positive and clear, distractions don't stand a chance. You're in the zone like a video game character focused on winning. You'll stay on track and crush your goals like a pro gamer taking down the final boss.

No regrets and greater life satisfaction

Life is like a colorful canvas, and positive self-talk is the paintbrush that adds the vibrant strokes of happiness. When you embrace positivity, you see life through a kaleidoscope of bright possibilities. You're more grateful for the little things and find joy in the simplest of moments. And you're not afraid to step out of your comfort zone, which means you can live life the way you were meant to. With a positive outlook, you'll create a masterpiece of a life characterized by satisfaction and contentment. And, as a bonus, there's a chance that you'll live a little longer than your grumpy neighbors. Studies show that optimistic people tend to live longer because they don't stress too much when life throws curveballs at them.

RECAP: POSITIVE SELF-TALK TO THE RESCUE!

Positive self-talk is like a forcefield that protects your mind and body. It boosts self-esteem, strengthens your immune system, and eases pain. Your heart dances with joy, and you become a mental powerhouse, able to conquer challenges with resilience. It builds better relationships and laser-like focus in everything you do. Embrace positivity for a vibrant, regret-free life full of satisfaction and true happiness.

REWRITING NEGATIVE SELF-TALK WITH POSITIVE AFFIRMATIONS

First off, it's important to know that you can't completely stop your thoughts. Every person's mind is busy, so it's always chatty. That's totally normal. While you can't stop your thoughts, you can definitely change how you talk to yourself. That's why some people look so miserable, and others look like they're about to indulge in the best ice cream ever—like every day.

Overcoming negative self-talk starts with self-awareness. You can only catch those thoughts in the act if you're aware of what's happening in your mind. With all the knowledge you've gained about self-awareness from the previous chapters, you've already laid a strong foundation for overcoming any negativity that may be haunting you. The next big step is to challenge your negative thoughts—

another skill you've already learned in the previous chapters. All you need to do now is practice and build on it, and you'll do that with a powerful mental tool called affirmations.

What are affirmations?

They're simply statements you say to yourself repeatedly. Affirmations can be negative ("You're so stupid!") or positive ("You're brilliant and it's OK to make mistakes."). To rewrite negative self-talk, you should turn your negative affirmations into positive affirmations. It's simple. It's powerful. And it can boost your confidence, self-esteem, and overall well-being. Think of positive affirmations as little pep talks you give yourself to create a positive and empowering mindset.

It may sound fluffy and perhaps a little awkward, but these guys are solidly backed by science. There's an entire branch of psychology dedicated to it, called self-affirmation theory.

It doesn't end there, though.

Neuroscientists were interested in finding out if affirmations have an effect on the brain's physiology, and it turns out they do! They've discovered that practicing positive affirmations increases specific neural pathways in the brain. So, yeah, positive affirmations really do work.

But there's a catch: They only work if you practice them regularly.

RECAP: THERE'S MAGIC IN AFFIRMATIONS

Or . . . There's science in affirmations (which is kind of the same thing!). You have the power to change how you think and feel about yourself by simply making positive statements about yourself. These statements are known as positive affirmations, and the key to success is regular practice.

Twenty positive affirmations you can start using right now

The best affirmations are the ones you come up with by yourself, for yourself, because you're unique and you have your own brand of love and light to share with the world. At the end of the chapter, I'll guide you on a fun activity to do just that. But since crafting your own positive affirmations can take some time, start by practicing any of the below statements in the meantime. Pick at least five that resonate with you the most, write them down, and start using them every day from this moment onward.

By the way, there's an interesting debate in the self-development community about whether affirmations are more effective when you state them in the first person (as in "I'm a math genius") or second person (as in "You're a math genius"). So, I'll leave the verdict up to you. Try your affirmations both ways and then self-reflect on which version really makes an impact on how you feel.

1. *I'm confident. I believe in my abilities and can achieve whatever I want.*
2. *I am loved and people care about me.*
3. *I'm not perfect, and that's OK because I'm good enough just the way I am.*
4. *I love my quirks and flaws. They make me unique.*
5. *I'm worthy of love and respect, even when I make mistakes.*
6. *My opinions matter and I have a right to speak up.*
7. *I don't have to be strong all the time—I'm allowed to feel angry or disappointed or scared.*
8. *I don't have to have all the answers to feel good about myself.*
9. *I'm grateful for what I have and I'm a generous person.*
10. *I value and respect other people just as much as I value and respect myself.*
11. *I have self-respect and don't have to compromise my morals for anyone.*
12. *I don't compare myself to others because we're all unique and special in our own right.*
13. *I'm an important part of my family.*
14. *I'm important to my friends.*
15. *I'm focused and fully capable of reaching my goals.*
16. *I love receiving help from other people when I can't figure things out on my own.*
17. *I'm courageous and can stand up for myself.*

18. *I love life, no matter what challenges it throws my way.*
19. *I am dependable.*
20. *I am a reliable friend all the time.*

END-OF-CHAPTER ACTIVITY: CREATE YOUR OWN AFFIRMATIONS

Step 1: Identify a negative thought.
Think about thoughts that have been holding you back or making you feel insecure. It could be that pesky voice saying, "I'm not good enough" or "I'll never succeed."

Step 2: Turn it into a positive affirmation.
Now, let's turn that negative thought upside down! Write down the positive opposite that counters your belief. For example, if you feel like "I'm not smart enough," change it to "I am intelligent and capable."

Step 3: Keep it short and sweet.
Short affirmations are super effective and easy to remember. You can even make it fun and catchy! For example, "I'm bold and unstoppable."

Step 4: Add emotion and make it present.
Make your affirmation come alive. Add some feeling to it by saying things like "I am excited about my potential" or "I feel confident in myself." Also, affirmations work best in the present tense, so be sure to use "I am" or "You are" statements.

Step 5: Repeat, repeat, repeat!
Repetition is the key to the success of positive affirmations, so commit to saying yours daily. You can write them on sticky notes and put them all over your room and in strategic places like your mirror for a daily reminder.

Step 6: Stay real and believe in yourself.
Make sure your affirmations feel real and achievable to you. If a certain affirmation feels too far-fetched, scrap it, or soften it with "I am open to the idea of . . ." or "I am willing to believe I can . . ."

Step 7: Bonus tip . . . Get inspired!
If you need some inspiration, check out lists of premade affirmations that suit your goals. You can find ideas online or in self-help books.

Always remember that self-talk is a powerful tool. It can shape your mindset and transform your life for the better or for the worse—which way it goes is totally up to you.

Life is so much better when it's filled with positive self-talk, so dump the negativity, embrace the magic of affirmations, and pave the way for a vibrant and fulfilling life. You've got the power to be your own biggest fan and achieve greatness—go for it!

Next, we'll tackle a biggie: dealing with social pressure. See you in Chapter 7.

CHAPTER 7
BEYOND THE CROWD – OVERCOMING SOCIAL PRESSURE

> " *"Be yourself because an original is worth more than just a copy."*
>
> SUZY KASSEM

WHAT IS SOCIAL PRESSURE?

So, you totally get that you're unique, and you really want to embrace that idea. It's a pretty big deal because, honestly, what's so special about being like everyone else? Yet there's this thing that's always urging you to do anything to fit in . . . You can't see it, you can't touch it, and you can't really describe it—but you can *feel* it.

It lingers in the air every time you're in class or hanging with your friends or doing something in public with your family. It makes you self-conscious, forces you to make sure you're dressed right, that your hair looks OK, or that you're saying the appropriate words and using the right tone of voice and lingo—even if it doesn't sound remotely like the regular you.

That feeling is called social pressure, and it's the beast of all confidence killers.

Social pressure is like an invisible force that pushes you to conform to other people's expectations against your will. And it's super easy to give in because if you don't, you risk disappointing people, being judged harshly, and even being made fun of and labeled as some coward or the spoilsport in the crowd.

It's a tough challenge that leaves you in a classical catch-22 situation: If you don't give in to social pressure, you get to stay true to yourself, but you might be left standing all alone. And if you go with the flow just to fit in, you betray your true self but at least you've got a spot in the crowd and people like you.

None of those sound like they can leave you feeling confident, do they?

Is social pressure your friend or foe?

The thing is; social pressure isn't black and white. There are gray areas, and if you know how to navigate them, your confidence will not only remain intact, but it will also flourish.

So, no, social pressure isn't all bad.

In fact, it's quite useful in giving you the bump you need to move outside of your comfort zone in some cases.

Take Ben . . . He's a good friend because he's always available to support his pals. They like spending time with him because, despite needing motivation like 99% of the time, he's actually a great sport. Ben isn't a big risk taker and is left to his own devices; he'd be home reading or playing video games every free second of his life.

But that's where social pressure saves the day.

His friends normally invite him on action-filled adventures like mountain biking and rock climbing. He always says no, and then they tease him about it. Most of the time, Ben gives in and goes along. On the rare occasion that he doesn't go along, his friends let the issue go, too, and they never judge or treat him differently when he sits out. But when Ben goes on the adventures, he actually ends up having immense fun. Lately, he's even been contemplating taking up mountain biking as a sport.

In Ben's case, the social pressure he's under is good for him, because it allows him to explore life outside of his comfort zone (reading and video games) and gives him the opportunity to discover more about himself. And, as it turns out, he enjoys the activities with his friends so much that he wants to take it further. Who knows, maybe he'll become a world champ in mountain biking or some other adrenaline-fueled sport. The fact is, if it weren't for social pressure, Ben would probably never have discovered this hidden passion.

On the other hand, social pressure has a dark side.

Remember Aubrey, your friend who wants to travel, but his dad wants him to go to law school? Let's say Aubrey is so afraid of disappointing his dad that he ignores what *he* wants to do and applies for law school.

He pushes through, but he's miserable. In time, he retreats into himself even more and doesn't even talk to you about the things he was once so passionate about. Now, if he told you he had discovered that becoming a lawyer is fantastic and that it turns out he's passionate about it just like his dad, that would be fine.

But he hates it.

And you can see it in his face and hear it in his voice . . . He's living someone else's life.

In Aubrey's case, bending under social pressure has resulted in a personal disaster for him. If he doesn't build the confidence to get himself out of that trap soon, his life can turn out pretty terrible.

There's an important point to make here, though, and that's the fact that Aubrey never talked with his dad about how he really feels. Aubrey just knows that his dad has this vision for him, and he believes that if he doesn't fulfill that vision, his dad will be disappointed and reject him. Mostly, though, parents just want their kids to be happy. They may have different ideas about what that "happy" should look like, but that doesn't mean they won't accept a different version.

You owe it to yourself and your parents to be open with them about your plans and dreams. And if you're honestly terrified of telling them, maybe try the *'Beat fear and anxiety before they beat you'* exercise at the end of Chapter 3 before having a chat with them. If that doesn't help, there's nothing wrong with confiding in a trusted teacher or another adult you look up to. They'll help you get through it in the best way possible.

RECAP: UNDER PRESSURE...

Social pressure is that incredibly strong urge you feel to conform to people's expectations and to fit in—no matter what. Depending on the nature of the social pressure, it can be good or bad for you. When it comes to family expectations, your best strategy is to be true to yourself and be very honest about your interests and passions with your parents.

How to know the difference between helpful social pressure and toxic social pressure

It's super important to realize that social pressure is not only an important part of your life right now, but something that will be a part of it pretty much forever. You can never avoid it, but you can manage and beat it. That's how you can stay confident and always stay true to yourself, no matter what.

A big part of navigating social pressure involves knowing when it can serve you and when it can sink you. Let's see how helpful social pressure differs from toxic social pressure.

What to look out for	Helpful social pressure	Toxic social pressure
Alignment with Personal Values	Encourages you to try new experiences, explore your interests, and step outside of your comfort zone while still aligning with your core values and beliefs.	Pushes you to act in ways that go against your values, beliefs, or ethical standards, causing internal conflict and discomfort.
Positive Growth vs. Negative Consequences	Leads to positive personal growth, self-discovery, and expanded horizons. It helps you discover hidden talents and passions, like in the case of Ben, who found a new interest in mountain biking.	Results in negative consequences for your mental, emotional, or physical well-being, like Aubrey, who experienced misery and lost touch with his true passions.
Respectful Boundaries	Respects your boundaries and allows you to say no without fear of judgment or ridicule. Your friends and peers understand and accept your choices, even if they differ from theirs.	Disregards your boundaries and insists on compliance without considering your feelings or preferences. It may involve manipulation, ridicule, or emotional blackmail to get you to conform.
Empowerment vs. Helplessness	Empowers you to make informed decisions for yourself, promoting independence and self-confidence.	Makes you feel helpless or trapped, as if you have no choice but to conform to others' expectations, leading to a loss of self-esteem.
Long-Term vs. Short-Term Impact	Positively impacts your life in the long run.	Provides short-term relief by fitting in momentarily, but it can have lasting negative effects on your self-esteem and emotional well-being.
Supportive vs. Destructive	Comes from friends or peers who genuinely care about your well-being and support your growth and happiness.	Originates from individuals or groups that seek to control or manipulate you for their benefit, often at the expense of your happiness and authenticity.
Open Communication	Encourages open communication and understanding among friends, allowing for honest discussions about differences and choices.	Thrives on secrecy and fear, discouraging open communication and authentic expression of thoughts and feelings.

WHERE DOES SOCIAL PRESSURE COME FROM?

Peer pressure

This is a big one when it comes to social pressure, and you've probably heard the term many times. It's when people (mostly your friends or peers your age) use all sorts of tactics to get you involved in activities. You may be reluctant to participate because you're not interested, or you've got a little fear of the unknown, or the idea may simply clash with your values and give you bad vibes.

Sometimes, peer pressure can motivate you to do better in school or try new things (like Ben), which can be excellent for your morale and confidence. But, watch out, because it can also be tricky when it leads you to take risks or do things that don't match with your true self (like Aubrey).

Repeat after me: Fitting in and pleasing others is *never* a good reason to buckle under peer pressure. If you do something, do it because you *want* to.

> "To live is to choose. But to choose well, you must know who you are and what you stand for, where you want to go and why you want to get there."
>
> KOFI ANNAN

An intense need to belong

As you grow up, friends become super important in your life. You want to belong and be accepted by your social circle, right? Nothing wrong with that.

Maybe you look up to your friends and feel the pressure to be like them. This is why self-reflection is so crucial. It can bring up questions like *"Why do I want to be like them so badly?"* If the answer is superficial, something along the lines of wanting to be cool like them or "just because," those aren't good reasons. Have you thought about the possibility that maybe they want to be more like you? Or that the reason they hang out with you is because they like you just the way you are? Being yourself is by far the coolest thing you can do! You already belong, and you're doing just fine.

Now, if your friends want you to change and will reject you if you don't, they're not really your friends, are they? *They* don't belong with *you*. You have every right to be yourself in all your glory, just like them.

Most of the time, though, friends aren't that nasty. Mostly, the fear that you don't belong is a lie from none other than your pesky self-doubt gremlin. You already know how to handle that guy (check back to Chapter 2 if you need a recap).

On the flip side, you may feel the need to be more like a friend who's disciplined and focused on their goals, or maybe they have a way of cruising through challenges with optimism. Those are fantastic qualities, so if you feel inspired to be more like your friend in that regard, go for it. But the trick is to cultivate the same qualities your friend has, *not* to copy their personality. It's like seeing something that resonates with you and thinking, "I should try that but with my own twist!"

Family and cultural expectations

Your family and cultural background also have a stake in the social pressure pie. The values, traditions, and family expectations you grew up with can greatly influence the choices you make. That's perfectly fine if they resonate with you, but sometimes, this pressure can push you to make decisions only because you feel obligated to conform to get a stamp of approval.

This kind of pressure is probably the toughest to overcome, because going your own way has the potential of creating a rift between you and the people you love the most, especially if your family values their legacy and traditions above everything else.

The best advice in this regard is this: First, remember that you're the one who has to live with your choices for the rest of your life—not your family. Second, never underestimate the power of communication. If you can be crystal clear about your interests, passions, and expectations from life, your family will very likely want to see you excel in that—even if they don't agree or understand.

School

This ties in with cultural and family pressure because it has a lot to do with what you believe people expect of you. The drive to do well in classes, sports, or extracurricular activities can put a big load of pressure on your shoulders.

To take some of that load off, review your sports and extracurricular activities. Are you doing them because you love it or need it for your future, or because you think it's expected of you? If you're doing things that aren't enriching your existence or securing your future, just stop!

Seriously, life is too short to please other people at the expense of your own peace and happiness.

If you're doing everything you love and you still feel overwhelmed, an easy fix is to prioritize and schedule. You'll be amazed at the free time that appears out of thin air when you practice a little discipline in your daily life.

Social media

Remember comparisonitis from Chapter 2? Social media is the biggest source of social pressure that exists today. In addition to fighting the urge to compare yourself with the online versions of your friends and peers, you have to deal with endless ads about what's hot and not.

Don't be fooled.

The people who create ads and targeted posts are psychology buffs who know how to get inside your head and make your self-doubt gremlin take notice. Challenge what you see in the same way you challenge your negative thoughts. Are they true? Does your life really depend on going with that flow? Or is it a plot to suck the uniqueness out of you?

Remember, if you do what everybody else is doing, you might just as well be a soulless robot. Social media gives all of us a skewed perception of life. Go out there, mingle, and you'll soon see that most people don't even remotely represent all the stuff you see online.

RECAP: SOURCES OF SOCIAL PRESSURE

Social pressure can come at you from every angle, but the biggest one you should be aware of is social media. Other sources are your need to fit in, peer pressure, school, and expectations from your family.

THE CONNECTION BETWEEN SOCIAL PRESSURE AND YOUR MENTAL HEALTH

At your age, you're especially vulnerable to the effects of social pressure on your mental health because you're still discovering the real you—the authentic person you want to become one day. If you can't manage social pressure and resist it when necessary, it can make you feel like someone's playing yo-yo with your mind and identity. You'll soon feel lost and disconnected from yourself, and that can open the doors to stress, anxiety, and even depression.

In 2019, a British investigative program revealed that a whopping 68% of young people (aged 16 to 30) thought they could have mental health issues. But that's not the worst part. Apparently, many teens have gotten so used to feeling down that they might not even realize they're experiencing anxiety and depression symptoms, and 37% of young people don't feel confident. On the other hand, there has been so much hype around mental health issues that a staggering number of teens believe they have anxiety and depression when, in reality, they're just experiencing the motions of growing up. Many studies over the years have proven that there's a definite correlation between social pressure and mental health issues, especially for young people.

Point in case: Your sanity totally depends on your ability to overcome social pressure.

A PEEK INTO THE EFFECTS OF SOCIAL PRESSURE

Emotional overload

At the end of the day, we're social creatures, and we just want to love and be loved. But the pressure that comes with that desire can cause some intense emotions.

Sometimes, it can feel like you're constantly on edge, trying to keep up with what (you think) others want or think of you.

But here's a secret: Your mind is pretty resilient, and despite all the noise out there about mental health problems, it's not going to let you down that easily, especially if you nourish it with everything you've been learning in these pages. Take care of your precious mind, and I promise, it will take care of you.

A drowning self-esteem

This is that thing I talked about earlier about feeling disconnected from yourself. The influence of social pressure can make you think you have to mold your personality, interests, and beliefs to fit in. In serious cases, it can cause an identity crisis, where you're unsure of who you really are or what you genuinely value.

It's not a fun place to be in, so remind yourself every day that it's not only OK to embrace yourself and your unique qualities, but also a requirement for a confident life.

Struggles with your body image

Social pressure often revolves around appearance and body image and—you guessed it—social media dictates the pace here. Never, ever fall for those unrealistic beauty standards and expectations.

You're beautiful, handsome, gorgeous, and smokin' hot just the way you are. You tick all the right boxes, so go ahead and fall in love with what you see in the mirror! If you *want* to change anything, like maybe getting fitter or a little stronger, do it for the right reasons. Otherwise, move on, 'cause there's not one inch of yourself to be ashamed of.

Increased temptation to take part in risky behavior

Peer pressure can be a strong toxic motivator for engaging in things you'd normally not even think of. You might feel the pull to try substances, engage in dangerous stunts, or break rules just to fit in. Don't fall into this ditch. It doesn't have a bottom and the people who pushed you in won't hang around to throw you a lifeline. They're not your friends. Always use your critical thinking cap and consider the consequences of risky temptations very, very carefully.

Academic issues

The pressure to perform academically can have the opposite effect of what you hope or expect; it can eventually lead to burnout and bad grades. Then there's the whole juggling act between trying to maintain good grades, being superb in those extracurriculars, and being a decent friend. The key here is to find a way to balance all of it. Try different strategies and schedules until you find something that makes you feel more in control and chill.

Feeling isolated

Want to know what's weird? The harder you try to fit in, the more alone and uncertain you feel. It makes you stressed and anxious about being rejected or judged, and to avoid that, you simply withdraw and keep to yourself. Genuine and meaningful connections come from being yourself and finding people who appreciate you for who you are.

RECAP: HOW SOCIAL PRESSURE AFFECTS YOUR LIFE

From emotional distress to feeling tempted to do risky stuff, social pressure can make you feel like you're being pushed into a corner with no way out. There's a clear link between your mental health and experiencing social pressure, and if you can't fight it, life can get pretty depressing.

But that's not the end of the story, because you CAN fight back.

HOW TO OVERCOME SOCIAL PRESSURE

Meet your ultimate weapon: assertiveness

You know how sometimes you're too shy to speak up, and then later you're like "Ugh, why didn't I just say something!?" Or maybe you've seen someone who was way too pushy and in-your-face while talking to another someone, and your inner voice was like "Whoa . . . Take it down a notch!"

None of those are helpful in social interactions . . . You want to strike a balance between being a total pushover and being rude. That's where assertiveness comes in. Being assertive means you can express your thoughts, feelings, and needs in an honest and respectful way. You don't have to be afraid to share your ideas, ask for what you want, or disagree with someone. It's about knowing your worth and believing that your ideas matter as much as anyone else's. But at the same time, it's also about being open and respectful, and mindful of other people's opinions and feelings.

Assertiveness is a skill you can learn with some willpower and practice, so no worries if you're on the shy side. You've come a really long way since Chapter 1, and with all the skills you've gained so far, assertiveness will be second nature for you in no time.

The benefits of being assertive

You can help cultivate better understanding between yourself and other people

Don't you just hate it when someone doesn't get what you're saying? And then they turn around to tell you that you're the one who doesn't get them . . . It's so annoying, I know.

The real issue isn't comprehension. It's a lack of communication. For some reason, we tend to think other people are supposed to know what's going on in our heads. We talk to ourselves all the time, so we totally get ourselves, but when those words come out, they're not exactly articulate.

But when you're assertive, you don't assume the person you're talking to knows what you're thinking, so you make a point of expressing yourself well. And that makes you a great help, too, because it encourages them to do the same. Then, like magic, the two of you understand each other perfectly.

Less drama

Miscommunication is the biggest reason people bicker and fight. And then, as if we assume the other person has a hearing problem, we raise our voices to get the point across. But no matter how loud we go, they just don't get it . . .

Assertiveness comes with a level of tact you'll learn to appreciate; there's no need to yell, like ever. You'll be able to share your point of view calmly, respectfully, and crystal clear. It's by far the most effective way to prevent misunderstandings from turning into total blowouts. Conflict is stressful, and you don't need it in your life.

Getting your needs met

I bet you've felt the sting of having your needs overlooked or ignored. It really hurts. And it sucks. The thing is, it probably wasn't done on purpose. These things happen when people don't really know what you need. When you learn to be assertive, people are more likely to listen and respond positively. It's like opening the door to getting what you deserve and making sure your voice is heard.

Now that you've got the theory down, it's time to get practical and add assertiveness to your confidence-boosting toolbox so you can overcome social pressure.

RECAP: ASSERTIVENESS HAS THE LAST SAY

Assertiveness is the ultimate weapon against social pressure. It's a communication method that allows you to say exactly what you need, want, and expect—all while being a nice person who respects others.

How to be an assertive communicator

Make eye contact

When you're talking with someone, try to look them in the eye. It shows that you're confident and really engaged in the conversation. But don't stare them down like you're in a staring contest or anything—just keep it natural.

Use a strong but nonaggressive tone of voice

Your tone can change how your message comes across. So, when you're standing up for yourself or expressing your thoughts, use a firm tone that shows you mean business, but don't sound angry or pushy.

Be like "Hey, I've got something to say," not like "You better listen to me right now!"

Be mindful of your facial expressions

Your face can say a lot without you even realizing it. So, pay attention to your expressions. If you're trying to be assertive, keep a calm and composed face. Smiling is fine, but don't grin like you just heard a joke in the middle of a serious conversation.

Let your timing be perfect

You want to wait for the right moment to say something, even if it's very important. Don't try to nudge it into a busy or stressful situation, and make sure the other person isn't in a hurry. That way, they can give you their full attention. Also, when you're in the middle of the conversation, don't interrupt the other person. Listen and only reply when they're done.

Be specific

Always be clear when you're expressing yourself. Avoid vague language that can lead to misunderstandings and make sure the words coming out of your mouth are actually saying what you mean.

Be nonthreatening

Being assertive doesn't mean acting in an aggressive or scary way. Don't give off angry vibes, don't invade the other person's personal bubble, and stay away from threatening language. Just chill and be respectful.

Frame your messages positively

Use sensitive and constructive language and focus on keeping yourself cool and calm. Use words that show you want to find a solution or work things out. Be in control of your emotions. If the other person has some negative feedback, don't feel offended. Ask them to tell you more so you can deal with the issue objectively.

Use "I" statements

"I" statements keep the conversation personal, honest, and nonjudgmental. For instance, saying something like "I feel this way," or "I think we can do this," sounds much better than just throwing blame on the other person.

Be an active listener

Listening is just as important as talking. Give the other person your full attention. Show you care by nodding or making little noises to let them know you're following along.

Value yourself and your rights

Remember, you're wonderful, and you deserve to be treated with respect. Stand up for yourself and your rights, and don't let anyone walk all over you (but be decent about it).

Stay calm even if the other person overreacts or gives off negative vibes

Sometimes people can get all worked up, but that doesn't mean you have to join in on the drama. Your calmness can help diffuse tense situations.

Accept criticism and praise

Everyone has their ups and downs, and it's cool to take criticism and praise with an open mind because you can learn from both. Don't get hung up on criticism if you receive it—it's just another opportunity to grow and become better.

END-OF-CHAPTER ACTIVITY: GRAB A FRIEND AND HONE YOUR ASSERTIVENESS

Step 1: Find a partner.
First things first, find a friend who's down to improve their assertiveness with you. It can be someone you're close to, like your best friend, or someone you're comfortable with but haven't hung out with in a while. The important thing is that you both agree to support each other.

Step 2: Brainstorm assertiveness scenarios.
Now, brainstorm different scenarios where assertive communication would come in handy. These could be everyday situations, like deciding on what movie to watch, or more serious ones, like expressing your opinions in a group setting.

Step 3: Role-play.
Time to put on your acting hats! Review all the assertiveness techniques we discussed above and then take turns role-playing the scenarios you came up with. One of you will play the assertive communicator, while the other takes on the role of the other person in the situation.
Remember, this is just for practice, so feel free to have fun with it.
Switch roles every now and then.

Step 4: Give and receive feedback.
After each role-play, take a minute or two to give each other constructive feedback. Chat about what went well and what could be improved.

Step 5: Reflect and set goals.
When you're done practicing, take a moment to reflect on what you've learned. Discuss how it felt to practice assertive communication and what you both took away from the experience. Based on your reflections, set some personal goals for how you can be more assertive in your daily lives.

READY TO CHANGE SOMEONE'S LIFE?

Let's fulfill my promise to the man in the park with a bang! With your help, I can reach even more people, and he'll have had more of an impact than he'll ever know.

Simply by sharing your honest opinion of this book and a little about your own journey, you'll show other young people where to go to start their own story of improved confidence.

In under one minute, you can help others just like yourself by leaving a review! Thank you so much for your support. You're making more of a difference than you realize.

CONCLUSION

Confidence is the armor that shields you from doubt, the fuel that propels you forward, no matter what, and the light that guides your path.

High five to you for sticking around and exploring the world of confidence and self-discovery!

I hope you've found valuable insights and inspiration and that you're walking away with a new-found, unshakable confidence. Above all, I hope you'll embrace yourself from now on—all of you—because the world is such a better place with your uniqueness.

Throughout these pages, we've explored the importance of confidence as the key to navigating life's challenges and opportunities. You now know it's not a gift anyone is born with; it's a skill that can be cultivated through deliberate practice and an unwavering belief in your abilities. The power to shape your future is entirely in your hands, no matter your background or circumstances.

I shared my own experiences, as well as those of other teens, to offer you relatable perspectives and a guiding light. But now it's your turn. Embrace the journey ahead and whatever happens, stay true to yourself. The road may get bumpy and twisty, but I know you've got the right mindset to handle it like it's no one's business. You're strong and you can handle anything life throws at you. And remember, setbacks are the best opportunities to learn and grow.

As you navigate this exciting, weird, and wonderful ride called life, know that you're never alone. Seek support from friends, family, mentors, or even a kind stranger on a park bench (unless they look dodgy). Wherever you go, there will always be someone who believes in you and wants to see you thrive.

Your teenage years are a one-of-a-kind and a once-in-a-lifetime rite of passage, a perfect time to build a solid foundation for the future. Embrace the challenges, embrace yourself, and most importantly, have fun! Time has a way of flying by without you even noticing, so don't waste a second trying to please others or fitting in where you're not appreciated.

Remember, confidence is not about perfection; it's about accepting and believing in yourself—flaws, quirks, and all the rest.

REFERENCES

CHAPTER 1 REFERENCES

Abdou, A. (2021, August 5). The 2 types of confidence, according to science (and how to harness them). *Ladders | Business News & Career Advice.* https://www.theladders.com/career-advice/the-2-types-of-confidence-according-to-science-and-how-to-harness-them

Admin. (2021). Why is confidence so important? *MindBodySpirit Festival.* https://www.mbsfestival.com.au/healthy-living-hub/confidence-importance/

Confidence (for Teens) - Nemours KidsHealth. (n.d.). https://kidshealth.org/en/teens/confidence.html

Cullum, T. (2018, May 6). What is Social Confidence Anyway? - Todd Cullum - Medium. *Medium.* https://medium.com/@ToddCullum/what-is-social-confidence-anyway-8ca8f669d785

Eikenberry, K. (2012). The Confidence/Competence Loop. *The Kevin Eikenberry Group.* https://kevineikenberry.com/leadership/the-confidencecompetence-loop/

Espinosa, C. (2021). How The Confidence Competence Loop Can Benefit You. *Christian Espinosa.* https://christianespinosa.com/blog/how-the-confidence-competence-loop-can-benefit-you/

Happiful Magazine. (n.d.). Is Neuroscience the Key to Confidence? *Happiful Magazine.* https://happiful.com/is-neuroscience-the-key-to-confidence

Inc.Africa. (n.d.). https://incafrica.com/article/minda-zetlin-confidence-social-epistemic-julia-galef-how-to-build-confidence

Inc.Africa. (n.d.). https://incafrica.com/library/geoffrey-james-if-youve-got-this-1-character-trait-youll-probably-be-successful-according-to-neuroscience

Jenkins, P. (2023, July 4). Why Confidence Is Important (and How to Boost It) - Brilliantio. *Brilliantio.* https://brilliantio.com/why-confidence-is-important/

LinkedIn. (n.d.). https://www.linkedin.com/pulse/how-neuroscience-can-make-you-more-confident-malhotra-acc-cpcc/

The confidence – competence loop. (n.d.). https://www.carolynecrowe.co.uk/blog/the-confidence-competence-loop/

Today, P. (2023, June 26). Confidence. Psychology Today. https://www.psychologytoday.com/us/basics/confidence

Van Leeuwen, N. (2022). Two Concepts of Belief Strength: Epistemic Confidence and Identity Centrality. *Frontiers in Psychology, 13.* https://doi.org/10.3389/fpsyg.2022.939949

Wall, A. (2020, September 8). What Confidence is and is Not, and How to Get More of it in Your Life. *Athena.* https://www.athenastemwomen.org/post/what-confidence-is-and-is-not-and-how-to-get-more-of-it-in-your-life

What Confidence Is and Is Not - by Joyce Shafer. (n.d.). https://trans4mind.com/counterpoint/index-happiness-wellbeing/shafer17.html

CHAPTER 2 REFERENCES

Beresin, E., MD. (2022, June 3). Low Self-Esteem in Adolescents: What Are the Root Causes? Psychology Today. https://www.psychologytoday.com/intl/blog/inside-out-outside-in/202206/low-self-esteem-in-adolescents-what-are-the-root-causes

Bergagna, E., & Tartaglia, S. (2018). Self-esteem, social comparison, and Facebook use. *Europe's Journal of Psychology, 14*(4), 831–845. https://doi.org/10.5964/ejop.v14i4.1592

Chong, J. (2023). Low self-esteem: The role of social comparison — The Skill Collective. *The Skill Collective.* https://theskillcollective.com/blog/low-self-esteem-social-comparison

MSEd, K. C. (2022). Social Comparison Theory in Psychology. *Verywell Mind.* https://www.verywellmind.com/what-is-the-social-comparison-process-2795872

Self-Confidence Starts Early. (n.d.). Urban Child Institute. http://www.urbanchildinstitute.org/articles/features/self-confidence-starts-early

Self-esteem and teenagers - ReachOut Parents. (n.d.). https://parents.au.

reachout.com/common-concerns/everyday-issues/self-esteem-and-teenagers

Sharma, I. (2021, April 16). Does Confidence Issues Stem From Your Childhood? - Blog - HealthifyMe. *HealthifyMe.* https://www.healthi fyme.com/blog/does-confidence-issues-stem-from-your-childhood/

Shawi, A. F. A., & Lafta, R. (2015). Relation between childhood experiences and adults' self-esteem: A sample from Baghdad. *Qatar Medical Journal, 2014*(2). https://doi.org/10.5339/qmj.2014.14

Sma-Admin. (2022, April 11). *3 Causes of Low Self-Esteem in Teens (And What to Do About It) - Stop Medicine Abuse.* Stop Medicine Abuse. https://stopmedicineabuse.org/blog/details/3-causes-of-low-self-esteem-in-teens-and-what-to-do-about-it/

CHAPTER 3 REFERENCES

Account, S. (2022). 3 Things Your Teens Fear the Most. *Focus on the Family.* https://www.focusonthefamily.com/parenting/3-things-your-teens-fear-the-most/

Anxiety (for Teens) - Nemours KidsHealth. (n.d.). https://kidshealth.org/en/teens/anxiety.html

Department of Health & Human Services. (n.d.). *Trauma and teenagers – common reactions.* Better Health Channel. https://www.betterhealth.vic.gov.au/health/healthyliving/trauma-and-teenagers-common-reactions

Miller, C., Bubrick, J., PhD, & Anderson, D., PhD. (2023). How Anxiety Affects Teenagers. *Child Mind Institute.* https://childmind.org/article/signs-of-anxiety-in-teenagers/

mindbodygreen. (2022, September 21). *10 Signs Fear Is Running Your Life (And How To Get Back On Track).* Mindbodygreen. https://www.mindbodygreen.com/articles/signs-fear-is-running-your-life

Pickhardt, C. E., PhD. (2013, November 11). Appreciating Fear in Adolescence. *Psychology Today.* https://www.psychologytoday.com/us/blog/surviving-your-childs-adolescence/201311/appreciating-fear-in-adolescence

Stieg, C. (2020, March 20). How fear influences your behavior, and how to cope. *CNBC*. https://www.cnbc.com/2020/03/20/how-fear-influences-your-behavior-and-how-to-cope.html

SupaduDev. (2023). 4 Fear-Based Routines That Get You Stuck. *New Harbinger Publications, Inc.* https://www.newharbinger.com/blog/self-help/4-fear-based-routines-that-get-you-stuck/

Tosh, D. (2023). How to Recognize That Fear is Driving Your Behaviour — Phoenix-Hearted Woman. *Phoenix-Hearted Woman.* https://www.phoenixheartedwoman.com/blog/how-to-recognize-that-fear-is-driving-your-behaviour

CHAPTER 4 REFERENCES

Bailey, J. R. (2022, March 21). *Don't Underestimate the Power of Self-Reflection.* Harvard Business Review. https://hbr.org/2022/03/dont-underestimate-the-power-of-self-reflection

Botelho, G. (2020, November 30). Building Self-Confidence Through Self-Awareness | HR Exchange Network. *HR Exchange Network.* https://www.hrexchangenetwork.com/employee-engagement/columns/building-self-confidence-through-self-awareness

Capp, K. M. B. (2023). Top 11 Benefits of Self-Awareness According to Science. *PositivePsychology.com.* https://positivepsychology.com/benefits-of-self-awareness/

Davenport, B. (2022). The Benefits Of Practicing Self-Reflection. *Mindful Zen.* https://mindfulzen.co/benefits-self-reflection/

Davis, D. M., & Hayes, J. A. (n.d.). What are the benefits of mindfulness. *https://www.apa.org.* https://www.apa.org/monitor/2012/07-08/ce-corner

Dowches-Wheeler, J. (2021). How Self-Awareness Builds Confidence — Bright Space Coaching | Leadership Development for Women. *Bright Space Coaching | Leadership Development for Women.* https://www.brightspacecoaching.com/blog/2018/6/20/how-self-awareness-builds-confidence

Eurich, T. (2023, April 6). *What Self-Awareness Really Is (and How to Cultivate It).* Harvard Business Review. https://hbr.org/2018/01/

what-self-awareness-really-is-and-how-to-cultivate-it

Habash, C. (2022). What is self-reflection? Why is self-reflection important? *Thriveworks.* https://thriveworks.com/blog/importance-self-reflection-improvement/

Humber River Health. (2022, January 27). *The Benefits of Self-Awareness - Humber River Health.* https://www.hrh.ca/2022/01/27/the-benefits-of-self-awareness/

Jennifer. (2023, March 2). 10 Benefits of Self Awareness And How it Can Impact Your Life −. . . *Contentment Questing.* https://contentmentquesting.com/benefits-of-self-awareness/

LinkedIn. (n.d.). https://www.linkedin.com/pulse/link-between-confidence-self-awareness-grant-henderson/

Mindfulness Definition | What Is Mindfulness. (n.d.). Greater Good. https://greatergood.berkeley.edu/topic/mindfulness/definition

Mindfulness for Your Health. (2022, July 15). NIH News in Health. https://newsinhealth.nih.gov/2021/06/mindfulness-your-health

MSEd, K. C. (2023). What Is Self-Awareness? *Verywell Mind.* https://www.verywellmind.com/what-is-self-awareness-2795023

Self Awareness & Confidence. (n.d.). https://www.ulster.ac.uk/employability/advice/digital-learning-hub/self-awareness-and-confidence

Self-Reflection 101: What is self-reflection? Why is reflection important? And how to reflect. | Reflection.app — Your guided journal for wellness and growth. (n.d.). https://www.reflection.app/blog/self-reflection-101-what-is-self-reflection-why-is-reflection-important

Self Reflection - Benefits, Importance, and How To Do It | Toggl Track. (n.d.). https://toggl.com/track/self-reflection/

Self-Reflection: Definition and How to Do It. (n.d.). The Berkeley Well-Being Institute. https://www.berkeleywellbeing.com/what-is-self-reflection.html

Smith, M., MA. (2023). Benefits of Mindfulness. *HelpGuide.org.* https://www.helpguide.org/harvard/benefits-of-mindfulness.htm

Staff, M. (2023). What is Mindfulness? *Mindful.* https://www.mindful.org/what-is-mindfulness/

What Is Self-Awareness, and Why Is It Important? (n.d.). https://www.betterup.com/blog/what-is-self-awareness

What Is Mindfulness? | Taking Charge of Your Health & Wellbeing. (n.d.).

Taking Charge of Your Health & Wellbeing. https://www. takingcharge.csh.umn.edu/what-mindfulness

CHAPTER 5 REFERENCES

Capp, K. M. B. (2023). How to Increase Self-Awareness: 16 Activities & Tools (+PDF). *PositivePsychology.com.* https://positivepsychology. com/building-self-awareness-activities/

Choosing Therapy. (2023). Mindfulness for Teens: How It Works, Benefits, & 11 Exercises to Try. *Choosing Therapy.* https://www. choosingtherapy.com/mindfulness-for-teens/

How the power of storytelling can change the course of your career. (2019, November 6). [Video]. NBC News. https://www.nbcnews.com/ better/lifestyle/what-self-awareness-how-can-you-cultivate-it-ncna1067721

Hughes, J. (2022). How to Cultivate Self-Awareness (And Why That's Important). *Elegant Themes Blog.* https://www.elegantthemes.com/ blog/business/how-to-cultivate-self-awareness

Mindfulness Exercises (for Teens) - Nemours KidsHealth. (n.d.). https:// kidshealth.org/en/teens/mindful-exercises.html

Our Top Mindfulness Activities For Teens. (2021, February 7). Tutor Doctor. https://www.tutordoctor.co.uk/blog/2021/february/our-top-mindfulness-activities-for-teens/

Tjan, A. K. (2015, February 11). *5 Ways to Become More Self-Aware.* Harvard Business Review. https://hbr.org/2015/02/5-ways-to-become-more-self-aware

CHAPTER 6 REFERENCES

Admin. (2020). 4 Benefits of Positive Affirmations. *HeadWay Clinic.* https://www.headwayclinic.ca/4-benefits-positive-affirmations/

Affirmations: What Are They and How Do They Work? (n.d.). https://www. familycentre.org/news/post/affirmations-what-are-they-and-how-do-they-work

Beau, A. (n.d.). How to Spot and Swap the 4 Types of Negative Self-

Talk. *Shine.* https://advice.theshineapp.com/articles/how-to-spot-
and-swap-the-4-types-of-negative-self-talk/

Footprints To Recovery Addiction Treatment Centers. (2021). 7 Ways
to Combat Negative Self-Talk. *Footprints to Recovery | Drug Rehab &*
Alcohol Addiction Treatment Centers. https://footprintstorecovery.
com/blog/combat-negative-self-talk/

Healthdirect Australia. (n.d.). *Self-talk.* What Is It and Why Is It
Important? | Healthdirect. https://www.healthdirect.gov.au/self-
talk

Helfand, E. (2022). The Benefits of Positive Affirmations. *Wellspring*
Center for Prevention. https://wellspringprevention.org/blog/the-
benefits-of-positive-affirmations/

Holland, K. (2020, June 27). *Positive Self-Talk: How Talking to Yourself Is a*
Good Thing. Healthline. https://www.healthline.com/health/posi
tive-self-talk

How To Stop Negative Self-Talk - Headspace. (n.d.). Headspace. https://
www.headspace.com/mindfulness/stop-negative-self-talk

Identifying Negative Automatic Thought Patterns. (n.d.). Stress &
Development Lab. https://sdlab.fas.harvard.edu/cognitive-reap
praisal/identifying-negative-automatic-thought-patterns

Inc.Africa. (n.d.). https://incafrica.com/library/yoram-solomon-3-
things-you-should-stop-doing-to-turn-on-your-creative-brain

Goldman, R. (2022, November 4). *Affirmations: What They Are and How*
to Use Them. EverydayHealth.com. https://www.everydayhealth.
com/emotional-health/what-are-affirmations/

Kristenson, S. (2022). How to Stop Negative Self-Talk: A 14-Step
Guide. *Happier Human.* https://www.happierhuman.com/stop-nega
tive-self-talk/

Moore, C. M. P. (2023). Positive Daily Affirmations: Is There Science
Behind It? *PositivePsychology.com.* https://positivepsychology.com/
daily-affirmations/

Monteleone, D. (n.d.). *Negative Self Talk - What is it and why does it*
matter? | Proactive Health & Movement. Proactive Health &
Movement. https://www.proactivehm.com.au/negative-self-talk-
what-is-it-and-why-does-it-matter/

Morris, S. Y. (2016, December 19). *What Are the Benefits of Self-Talk?*

Healthline. https://www.healthline.com/health/mental-health/self-talk

Richards, L. (2022, March 18). *What is positive self-talk?* https://www.medicalnewstoday.com/articles/positive-self-talk

Richard. (2022). Affirmations. *Clinical Hypnotherapy Cardiff.* https://www.clinicalhypnotherapy-cardiff.co.uk/affirmations/

Santos, J. (2021). 10 Positive Affirmations for Teens and Young Adults (Free Printables). *But First, Joy.* https://butfirstjoy.com/positive-affir mations-for-teens-young-adults/

Scott, E., PhD. (2022). The Toxic Effects of Negative Self-Talk. *Verywell Mind.* https://www.verywellmind.com/negative-self-talk-and-how-it-affects-us-4161304

Scott, S. (2023). 67 Positive Affirmations for Teens & Young Students. *Happier Human.* https://www.happierhuman.com/positive-affirma tions-teens/

Self-Talk. (2020, December 9) *Psychology Today.* https://www.psycholo gytoday.com/intl/basics/self-talk

The Power of Positive Self Talk (and How You Can Use It). (n.d.). https://www.betterup.com/blog/self-talk

T, M. (2017). 8 Dangers of Negative Self-Talk. *Makeda Pennycooke.* https://makedapennycooke.com/8-dangers-negative-self-talk/

Wignall, N. (2022). 10 Types of Negative Self-Talk (and How to Correct Them). *Nick Wignall.* https://nickwignall.com/negative-self-talk/

CHAPTER 7 REFERENCES

Anxiety on the Rise: Are Societal Pressures to Blame? (2016, August 23) *Destination Hope - Your Destination for Recovery.* https://destination hope.com/anxiety-rise-societal-pressures-blame/

Hazlegreaves, S. (2019). Social pressure is damaging the mental health of millennials. *Open Access Government.* https://www.openaccessgov ernment.org/social-pressure-mental-health-of-millennials/70437/

Lautieri, A. (2019). Social Pressures Influence Mood And Behavior.

MentalHelp.net. https://www.mentalhelp.net/adolescent-develop ment/social-pressures-mood-and-behavior/

Peer Pressure (for Teens) - Nemours KidsHealth. (n.d.). https://kidshealth. org/en/teens/peer-pressure.html

Peer pressure or influence: pre-teens and teenagers. (2021, November 3). Raising Children Network. https://raisingchildren.net.au/teens/ behaviour/peers-friends-trends/peer-influence

Scripps Health. (2023, April 7). How Does Peer Pressure Affect a Teen's Social Development? *Scripps Health.* https://www.scripps.org/ news_items/4648-how-does-peer-pressure-affect-a-teen-s-social-development

Teens and Peer Pressure - Children's Health. (n.d.). https://www.childrens. com/health-wellness/helping-teens-deal-with-peer-pressure

Wpa. (n.d.). Social Anxiety, Social Media and your Mental Health. *WPA.* https://www.wpa.org.uk/health- wellbeing/articles/social-anxiety

REVIEW PAGE REFERENCES

Liles, M. (2022, October 10). *Parade.com.* parade.com. https://parade. com/989608/marynliles/confidence-quotes/

Made in the USA
Las Vegas, NV
15 November 2023

80745444R10098